ESSENCE OF THE DHAMMAPADA

THE WISDOM OF INDIA

Essence of the Bhagavad Gita
Essence of the Dhammapada
Essence of the Upanishads

Essence of the

DHAMMAPADA

The Buddha's Call to Nirvana

EKNATH EASWARAN

NILGIRI PRESS

© 2013 by The Blue Mountain Center of Meditation
All rights reserved. Printed in Canada
First printing August 2013

ISBN : 978–1–58638–097–7
Library of Congress Control Number: 2013931152

Printed on 100% post-consumer recycled paper

Cataloging-in-Publication Data will be found
on the last page of this book.

Nilgiri Press is the publishing division of the Blue Mountain
Center of Meditation, a nonprofit organization founded
by Eknath Easwaran in 1961. The Center also offers retreats
based on the eight-point program of passage meditation that
Easwaran developed and practiced. For information please
visit www.easwaran.org, call 800 475 2369 (USA) or
707 878 2369 (international and local), or write:
The Blue Mountain Center of Meditation,
Box 256, Tomales, CA 94971–0256, USA.

◇ Table of Contents

◇

This book has been produced by Eknath Easwaran's senior editors, longtime students who worked closely with him since his first book in 1970 and were charged by him with continuing to compile his books from transcripts of his talks after his passing.

In his last editorial planning meeting, in 1998, Easwaran gave instructions about the books in progress that he wanted completed from his unpublished transcripts, outlines, and notes. ESSENCE OF THE DHAMMAPADA *is the second of those posthumous projects to be published: the legacy of a gifted teacher sharing his immersion in a sacred text, conveyed in his talks and informal sessions with some of his closest students.*

It was Easwaran's longstanding desire to publish his commentary on the scripture that he felt contained the direct inspiration of the Buddha's words. It is a privilege to bring out this book for his readers around the world.

◇ *The Wisdom of India*

SOME YEARS AGO I translated what I called the classics of Indian spirituality: the Upanishads, the Bhagavad Gita, and the Dhammapada. These ancient texts, memorized and passed from generation to generation for hundreds of years before they were written down, represent early chapters in the long, unbroken story of India's spiritual experience. The Upanishads, old before the dawn of history, come to us like snapshots of a timeless landscape. The Gita condenses and elaborates on these insights in a dialogue set on a battlefield, as apt a setting now as it was three thousand years ago. And the Dhammapada, a kind of spiritual handbook, distills the practical implications of the same truths presented afresh by the Compassionate Buddha around 500 B.C.

These translations proved surprisingly popular, perhaps because they were intended not so much to be literal or literary as to bring out the meaning of these documents for us today. For it is here that these classics come to life. They are not dry texts; they speak to us. Each is the opening voice of a conversation which we are invited to join – a voice that expects a reply. So in India we say that the meaning of the scriptures is only complete when this call is answered in the lives of men and women like you and me. Only then do we see what the scriptures mean here and now. G. K. Chesterton once said that to understand the Gospels, we have only to look at Saint Francis of Assisi. Similarly, I would say, to grasp the meaning of the Bhagavad Gita, we need look no farther than Mahatma Gandhi, who made it a guide for every aspect of daily living. Wisdom may be perennial, but to see its relevance we must see it lived out.

In India, this process of assimilating the learning of the head into the wisdom of the heart is said to have three stages: *shravanam, mananam,* and *nididhyasanam;* roughly, hearing, reflection, and meditation. These steps can merge naturally into a single daily activity, but they can also be steps in a journey that unfolds over years. Often this journey is begun in response to a crisis. In my own case, though I must have heard the scriptures many times as a child, I don't remember them making any deep impression. When I discovered the Bhagavad Gita, I was attracted by the beauty of its poetry; I didn't understand its teachings at all. It was not until I reached a crisis of meaning in my mid-thirties, when outward success failed to fill the longing in my heart, that I turned to these classics for wisdom rather than literary beauty. Only then did I see that I had been, as the

Buddha puts it, like a spoon that doesn't know the taste of the soup.

Since that time I have dedicated myself to translating these scriptures into daily living through the practice of meditation. The book in your hands is one fruit of this long endeavor. Such a presentation can only be intensely personal. In my translations I naturally let the texts speak for themselves; here I make no attempt to hide the passion that gave those translations their appeal. To capture the essence of the Gita, the Upanishads, and the Dhammapada, I offer what I have learned personally from trying to live them out in a complex, hurried world. I write not as a scholar, but as an explorer back from a long, long voyage eager to tell what he has found.

Yet however personal the exploration, these discoveries are universal. So it is not surprising that at the heart of each of these classics lies a myth – variations on the age-old story of a hero in quest of wisdom that will redeem the world. In the Upanishads, a teenager goes to the King of Death to find the secret of immortality. In the Gita, standing between opposing armies on the eve of Armageddon, the warrior-prince Arjuna seeks guidance from an immortal teacher, Sri Krishna. And behind the Dhammapada lies the story of the Buddha himself, a true story woven into legend: a prince who forsakes his throne to find a way for all the world to go beyond sorrow in this life. These old stories are our own, as relevant today as ever. Myth always involves the listener. We identify with its heroes; their crises mirror ours.

Their stories remind us not only what these scriptures mean but why they matter. Like the texts themselves, they seek a response in our own lives.

So this book is both the fruit of a journey and an invitation. If you like, you may read it as a traveler's tale rich in the experience of some distant place, enjoying the sights and adventures without the travail of actually making the trip yourself. But this place is really no more distant than the heart, so if you find that this description calls you to your own voyage of exploration, my highest purpose in writing will be fulfilled.

◇ Introduction

IT WAS MANY years ago that I fell in love with the Buddha – not as a god, not as an angel, but as a man who was the finest flower of our five-thousand-year-old Indian civilization. There are many reasons to love the Buddha and to want to be like him, but most of all I was drawn to him because he fulfilled the long, long journey of human evolution. In his language, he reached the end of the way; he crossed the river of life.

Why did this man, born a prince named Siddhartha into whose lap the gods poured all their gifts, turn his back on everything that means so much to every one of us? In the age-old way of India's saints and sages, he went in search of the answer to a question that has tormented humanity since the dawn of creation: Is there no way to cross the river of life, from a world of change and separateness to a far shore of unity, joy, and peace?

Once he began to seek an answer, Siddhartha did not rest until he found it. For six long years he searched and struggled, inflicting heroic experiments upon his body and mind. He would not go by what tradition had handed down: he would not accept what theology taught; he would not even trust reason and intellect. There was only one way in which he could know the truth, and that was to realize it for himself through hard self-discipline and even harder experience. For the Buddha, religion did not mean theology, metaphysics, dogma, or even faith. He sought personal experience, personal realization, which he finally achieved on the night of his enlightenment under the bodhi tree.

When Prince Siddhartha came into this life there was only a thin veil of illusion separating him from full enlightenment. He was born in the royal Shakya line, in a beautiful area at the foot of the Himalayas, destined to inherit his family's warrior tradition. As a young man he was taught by the best teachers and became proficient in the arts of peace and war, a superb horseman and archer. As a youth he was surrounded with all the pleasures of life: palaces, gardens, music, and dance. With a loving and beautiful wife, he had a son who promised to continue the royal tradition. All this Prince Siddhartha had, and yet nothing would satisfy him. All these appeared so small to him because, after many lifetimes of seeking, it was his destiny to reach the end of the way in this life, and to become the teacher of countless millions.

More than twenty-five hundred years ago, on the full-moon night in the month of May, the young prince became the

Buddha. On that night Prince Siddhartha awoke from the long sleep of separateness in which all of us are still dreaming and became the Buddha, the Awakened One. This tremendous experience is the foundation for everything that came afterward. All of the Buddha's teachings rest on this supreme experience of awakening. Afterwards, for forty-five years the Buddha wandered all over the dusty paths of northern India, showing everyone – prince and pauper, beggar and merchant, young and old, man and woman, householder and mendicant – the life-fulfilling way beyond suffering. Wanting to preserve his priceless words, his disciples collected his teachings in the Pali Canon, memorized and passed down from generation to generation until written down in the first century B.C. A part of the Pali Canon, the Dhammapada conveys the Buddha's teaching in vivid, practical verses that use the everyday language of the villagers rather than the lofty discourse of the priests. In time, as Buddhism spread throughout Asia, the Dhammapada became a much-loved scripture translated into many languages, from Tibetan to Chinese. Wherever the message of the Buddha traveled, the Dhammapada became a kind of spiritual handbook.

In this handbook we are going right to the source, to the very words of the Buddha. Where the teachings of the Buddha are concerned, there is a lot of tradition, a lot of teaching not from the Buddha but from his followers – some useful, some spiritual, some scholarly, and some neither scholarly nor spiritual. But the Dhammapada, I believe, must have come from the Buddha there is only one like the Buddha, who threw a crown away and put on the faded robes of a mendicant.

"Through the dharma I turn the wheel that rules the whole world, the wheel of the law." The wheel of the law of love set in motion by the Buddha may never be stayed. It will go on and on. Wherever war is waged, however selfish people become, the teaching of the Buddha will inspire ordinary men and women because, once like us, he transcended all human conditioning and fulfilled human evolution.

From the human point of view, then, there are two Buddhas: one, Prince Siddhartha Gautama who became the Buddha, and the other, the Buddha principle: impersonal, inexpressible, eternal. We need the human Buddha, who lives as we do, talks as we do, laughs as we do, weeps as we do. We respond to the man, so accessible, so personal, so tender, and we are inspired to follow in his footsteps. Yet by virtue of illumination the Buddha has gone beyond personality, beyond individuality.

In a few of the magnificent representations of the Buddha, he is not shown at all. We see only an empty seat. There is nobody there. It's the perfect image, because the eternal Buddha cannot be described. How can we describe in human language the Awakened One, free from all conditioning? How can we describe a man or woman who has become universal, who will always act in freedom? Such a person is not individual, not personal. He or she has become an eternal force which can come to life in every one of us.

We are drawn irresistibly to the Buddha because we all respond deeply to goodness and wisdom. We may say we do not believe in God, we may say we don't follow the spiritual life, but everywhere people are searching for someone leading a selfless, loving life. When we see someone who can suffer patiently under attack, remain calm in the midst of turmoil, and return good will for ill will, we feel an innate attraction.

Such people shine like the Himalayas. When you approach the Himalayas from the dusty plains of India, you see a glorious sight you can never forget. Just so the Buddha's appeal will never change. The Buddhist scriptures are lavish in their praise for their great teacher, the Tathagata, "the one who has understood things as they are," because after all the tributes were paid, his disciples felt there still remained about the Buddha a core that was unknown, an essence of mystery. Words could not express it because thoughts could not follow. Even after twenty-five hundred years, we are forced to agree with the words of the disciples: "Deep is the Tathagata, immeasurable, incomprehensible as the sea."

The Buddha combined within himself two extraordinary qualities seldom seen in the same person. On the one hand, he was a man of rich and responsive human sympathy, of unfailing patience, infinite gentleness, and universal good will. On the other hand, he had an intellect as sharp as a razor's edge. He seems to have combined within himself the two almost conflicting roles of a passionate lover of mankind and a philosophic genius, harmonized beautifully into one single radiant personality.

The Buddha had a well-trained intellect but he never drew attention to it. He would never enter into arguments and could never be drawn into a controversy, choosing to maintain what the commentaries call a "noble silence." On one occasion, a few of his disciples began to doubt. Maybe their teacher didn't have the answers after all. "Perhaps the Blessed One is afraid of engaging in philosophical disputes?" they asked.

"The very thought that I could be defeated in argument," the Buddha replied, "is impossible." He would not be drawn into futile discussions that have nothing to do with things as they are. By his very silence he taught: these questions are mere theories and dogmas.

The Buddha doesn't even ask us to believe in God. He asks us to cross the river of life and find the peace he called nirvana. He doesn't ask us to take anything on faith but proposes a grand experiment: step-by-step research into the depths of our consciousness. Because of this approach, the Buddha has been called an atheist, an agnostic, a nihilist. He was none of these; he was a supreme spiritual scientist. Ask him, "Is there a God?" and he will reply, "Why don't you enter the depths of your consciousness and see for yourself? The answer is right within you."

Everything is right within us. All the equipment is there. We must simply get in, close the door, and conduct the experiment. At the conclusion of the experiment, we will know for ourselves whether there is a God or not.

The Buddha is a tough teacher, which is the mark of any good spiritual guide. He isn't blind to our faults. Because he is a good friend, the Buddha uses strong words when it is necessary. The purpose of a good friend is not just to say nice things to us. A good friend will always do things that are helpful to us and give us loving criticism even though it may cause us some frustration, even some distress. It is speaking as an experienced guide and a good friend that the Compassionate Buddha inspires us, encourages us, and pushes us on.

Now we are almost ready to begin. We have a good teacher in the Buddha and the Dhammapada as our guidebook. But we need one thing more: stories. In the Buddhist and Hindu traditions, stories are used to encourage us on our journey, to warn us of dangers, obstacles, and enemies, and to lift our spirits when the going gets rough. Personal anecdotes and stories bring the lessons home. They bring what could be empty metaphysics and philosophy down from the clouds to the kitchen, the office, the store.

Stories are the way we can get to know the Buddha as a living figure, and stories bring what could be a dull concept to life. So I will follow this method, using stories to bring out the warmth and humanity of these teachings – to bring the wisdom of the scriptures down from the head into the heart.

When, in course of time, institutions become rigid and beliefs become mere shells, a great teacher arises to put new life into old wisdom and new meaning into eternal laws by demonstrating them in his or her own life. In this manner, the Buddha brought renewal to the Vedic tradition of India. But his words apply equally to all – Buddhists, Hindus, Christians, Jews, Moslems, and agnostics – because these truths are timeless and universal. The words of the Buddha speak directly to our hearts.

◆

ESSENCE OF THE DHAMMAPADA

◇ *Should I Go?*

ALONG THE RIVER the boatmen cry, *Who is going across? Who is going across?* This is the song of the ferrymen who would row us to the other shore. And the Buddha, too, the eternal boatman, calls to us, *Is there anyone who wants to go to the other shore, to nirvana?* We have heard the boatman beckon, but the water is high, the waves are rough. We hesitate. Yet we cannot turn away. How can we ignore the cry of the Buddha, who can take us across the turbulent, treacherous sea of life? How can we shut our ears to his promise that in the limitless sea of change there is an island, a farther shore: nirvana, a realm utterly beyond the transient world in which we live?

We are all moving towards nirvana, the Buddha says. No one will ever be lost. Everyone will get home one day. Yet most of us hesitate when we hear the summons. We could take our evolution into our hands, here and now, but we waver. Instead of waiting for the forces of evolution to buffet us for a million years, instead of waiting for our heart to be broken a million times, we could try, during this very life, to take command of our destiny. But the journey seems too long, the effort too arduous.

We'll wait and go another day. There is too much to do on this shore. We are not ready.

Yet for a few special creatures, a time comes when they say, "All right, I'm coming! Don't leave without me!" They don't want to wait any longer. They want to make the journey *now*.

Others say, "Let me see what happens if I get into the boat . . ." They have one foot on the shore and the other in the boat – when the Buddha gives them a push. Either way, whether you jump in or are pushed, you are in the boat and on your way.

> *Few are those who reach the other shore; most*
> *people keep running up and down this shore.*
>
> *But those who follow the dharma, when it has*
> *been well taught, will reach the other shore,*
> *hard to reach, beyond the power of death.*
> [85–86]

WE DO NOT know it, but the Buddha does: we were born for this adventure. As long as we are running up and down on this shore, we are not aware of our real needs. We think a handful of profit or a thimbleful of praise will satisfy us. It is only when we open our ears to the Buddha's call that we begin to understand that nothing will satisfy us except this great journey. It is our deepest desire, our grand destiny, to reach the end of the long travail of human evolution.

To emerge from the world of change into nirvana is what the Buddha means by crossing the river of life. Coming close to the language of modern science, the Buddha teaches that everything is in flux: nothing is the same; everything changes. The word used in both Hinduism and Buddhism is *samsara,* "to move with terrible intensity." Everything is moving, flowing, coming into existence and passing away. No one can find a firm

foothold anywhere on this shore – not in any personal attachment, not in any personal achievement – because everything is
changing, body, mind, and world. So, he asks, who is ready to go
across to the other shore?

The Buddha's cry is so urgent because there is very little time
to make experiments in life. There is very little time in which to
learn. Sixty years, seventy years, even a hundred years, pass in
the twinkling of an eye. There is no time to quarrel. There is no
time to misunderstand. There is no time to be selfish.

On this shore life is over so quickly, and then we shed the
mortal body, but the Buddha calls us with the promise of a life
beyond suffering:

> For those in great fear of the flood, of growing old and of
> dying – for all those, I say, an island exists where there
> is no place for impediments, no place for clinging: the
> island of no going beyond. I call it nirvana, the complete
> destruction of old age and dying.

We all hear this message. For some it comes like an express
delivery in the night. Others hear a whisper so quiet they easily
ignore it. For a few one postcard is enough. They know it's time
to seek what is permanent, what really matters. For some the
postcard comes when they are young. More often it comes to
the middle-aged. For some it comes after old age has brought
wisdom. For the Buddha it came when he was a young man,
with everything that life could offer.

Siddhartha Gautama – Siddhartha means "he whose wishes
are fulfilled" – was born in a royal family in a small kingdom on
the border of the mountain state of Nepal, about two hundred
miles from the sacred city of Benares. At his birth, so the story

goes, a wise sage foretold that this boy would either become a great emperor or a great teacher, and the king, his father, like a good king, wanted his son to become an emperor, so the little prince was always carefully protected from any sorrow that might bring him to question the pursuit of power and wealth.

Then one day, when he was twenty-nine, the prince asked to be taken outside the palace. There he saw the four sights that were to change his own life and the lives of all Asia for thousands of years to come: an old man, a sick man, a dead man, and a mendicant seated in meditation – visions of decay, disease, death, and deliverance. It was almost as if a bomb exploded within the young man at the sight of the fate that lies in store for every human being. Day and night, one question began to torment him: "Is there no way to be free from the ruthless tyranny of disease, decay, and death?"

This question would not let him sleep. It would not let him rest. All the pleasures of the table lost their appeal. The twinkling feet of the dancing girls, the magic lilt of the vina, became meaningless to his eyes and ears. The roses nodding their heads in the breeze in the royal garden, the gleaming snows melting on the peaks of the mighty Himalayas, all these now began to cry out to him of the fleeting shadow play that is your life and mine.

Unable to bear this torture any more, one full-moon night in the month of May the prince stole into the royal chamber where his wife and baby son were sleeping peacefully side by side. He did not wake them up but pronounced a blessing on them. Then he left the royal chamber silently, called his loyal charioteer Channa, and told him to saddle his favorite horse. Quietly, the prince and Channa rode out of the palace.

At dawn they reached a desolate forest, where Siddhartha ordered Channa to exchange clothes with him, royal robes for a simple garment. Then he asked Channa to return to the palace and break the news that he had gone in search of an answer to the question, "Is there no way to transcend change and death?" This is the question that burst in his consciousness – not when he was an old man but at the pinnacle of youth, with all the wealth and power of his father's kingdom at his command.

It was the vision of impermanence that pushed him to leave his wife and son, not selfishly, but out of infinite compassion, a compassion so profound that it is almost beyond our human understanding. Six years later, when he had found the way to cross the river of life, he didn't withdraw forever into the forest, but returned to rescue them so that they too could discover what lies beyond the world of change and death.

WHEN I WAS a boy, in my own small way I received the same message young Siddhartha had been given so many hundreds of years ago. It was my grandmother, who was my spiritual teacher, who delivered this postcard to me. This illiterate lady planted the seeds of mystical awareness in the depths of my consciousness before I reached the age of sixteen. She opened a window in my consciousness, saying, "Look! If you look far enough you'll see Yama, the King of Death, waiting for you." My grandmother loved me passionately, and this was a great blessing she bestowed on me when I was a boy, which I did not understand at that time.

In my ancestral village, my extended family occupied one

small lane, with homes on either side where more than a hundred people lived. Death was often a visitor to our lane, and deaths almost always occurred at home. In the larger houses there was a small alcove called "the dark room," and it was the tradition to keep the body there overnight before the cremation the following day. That room was never used for any other purpose.

Even the bravest men in my home would never walk past that room at night, because for us Yama lived there; death lived there. When anyone died, the body was taken to that room and placed on the floor with an oil lamp lit nearby. In these oil lamps the wick must be pushed forward into the oil as it burns, and this has to be done many times during the night. Whatever happened, the lamp couldn't be allowed to go out, since this was considered to be part of the funeral ritual.

My grandmother would volunteer to do this. Not only was she willing, she would lie by the side of the dead body – the body of someone she had known all of her life, often someone for whom she had had great affection – and fall asleep as usual, waking up when it was necessary to tend to the lamp. I was amazed; I couldn't understand how she could do this. Only now do I understand that it was because she knew that body was just an empty garment, the poor jacket that the person had shed. Would you be afraid of a jacket? For her it was that obvious, but I didn't understand until many, many years later, when I went so deep in meditation that spiritual wisdom finally drove out fear.

My grandmother wasn't good at explaining things with words, but she loved me so much that she wanted me to make the central question of my life not how to be successful, not how to make money, but how to conquer this sad fate that awaits everybody – man, woman, and child. Today after more than fifty years I remember one of her lessons. On the front page of today's paper, there was a picture of a little boy of five being carried in the arms of a lifeguard. The boy had been swept away by the waves at the beach and could not be rescued in time, even though many tried. Just a glance at the photo sent a message deep into my heart. It was with me throughout the day, it was with me throughout the night, as I recalled a similar scene that took place in my village half a century ago when a boy I knew drowned in the river nearby. I was with my mother, who almost broke down, and my grandmother. The sorrow was too much to bear because we knew the boy; we knew the parents. When we returned home I could hardly speak.

That afternoon, my grandmother sat by my side and talked to me just as the Buddha would have talked. She didn't try to console me. She tried to strengthen me. She knew my heart was open and she struck hard, "This is going to happen to everybody. All relationships are going to come to an end." She specified: grandmother and grandfather, father and mother, parents and son, parents and daughter, brother and sister, friend and friend. My mother, who was the gentlest, most compassionate woman said, "I don't want to hear," which is the natural, human response. I didn't have a reputation for being a brave boy, but somehow my granny's grace came to me at that moment. I told her I wanted to hear more. I wanted to understand. "This is what I want to rescue you from," she replied. At that time, I couldn't understand. Only much later did I realize that she was trying to give me the courage I would need to take to the spiritual life.

My grandmother's message was the same as the Buddha's: Even if you are young, make this the central question of your life, and always remember this is waiting for everyone. Because of her, it became a vital issue with me even before I undertook the practice of meditation when I was nearing middle age.

Millions of people have read the words of the Buddha, millions read the Hindu scriptures, but my grandmother opened the window through which I could see, "Oh, yes! There is Yama waiting." Now, because of the grace of my teacher, I can say to Yama, "You cannot conquer me."

To me, this is the greatest love. As the Buddha says, this is the greatest gift. It is the measure of the Buddha's infinite love and compassion that he wants every one of us to enter nirvana in this very life. Then Yama steps aside. When we pass by he says, "I have no power over you."

BEFORE WE EMBARK on this adventure to cross the river of life, a certain amount of experimentation is necessary. Without experimenting in some reasonable measure with the manifold attractions of the world, I don't think ordinary people like us can get the incentive to make this journey. We must have some capacity for looking at ourselves and at life with a practical wisdom, with a degree of detachment that usually comes only after we have tasted what life has to offer. But if we have some capacity to observe ourselves and to assess our experiences, I think any man or woman of reason can see that we cannot find our fulfillment in the external world. Our security can never be guaranteed by leaning on external props.

This kind of wisdom does not come through the intellect but through experience, often as we enter our thirties and forties. At that time most sensitive people will look back upon their earlier years and ask a pointed question: "Has all this wandering up and down this shore had any meaning?" Finally, under the blows and ruthless pressure of life, every thoughtful person will ask, "Is all I am going through real? Or am I dreaming?" We come into the world from no one knows where, grow up from childhood to youth, pass from middle age into old age, and then finally depart to no one knows where. Is this life real? Or are we the stuff that dreams are made of? The answer given by the intellect is blunt, "Life has no meaning, no purpose. Don't even think of attaining nirvana. Just stay where you are and have a good time – if you can."

For the determined person, this answer is not enough. Such a person will be haunted by questions: What, exactly, am I holding on to for security, for meaning? In the midst of change is there anywhere to stand firm? To know that happiness cannot come from anything outside, and that all things that come into being have to pass away: this is what the Buddha calls right understanding, the beginning of wisdom.

It's a poignant moment when we first realize that our own body is as fragile as a flower, as light as the wisps of foam tossed by the waves at the seashore, as ephemeral as a mirage. It's hard to believe that one day babies are going to be teenagers, then adults, then senior citizens. In India, a poor country, I was always shocked at what the passage of just ten years could do. I would welcome new students each year, amazed at how fresh they looked, almost with a morning dew on them. Then ten years later I would meet one of them in the bazaar. I would return their smile and chat with these old students, but it brought me much pain to realize how much they had changed.

Here, in a wealthy country, we may be able to prolong the youthful glow a little more, but this too can lead to problems. Everywhere we are cautioned to never let our true age reveal itself. I confess, my usual response is, "Why not? Let it reveal itself." Everywhere we are warned that if we let slip our true age, if we reveal that we are no longer in our twenties or, at the most, in our thirties, we are going to be unloved. Because it is simply impossible to cherish someone who is old.

> *Look on the world as a bubble; look on it as a mirage. Then the King of Death cannot even see you. Come look at this world! Is it not like a painted royal chariot? The wise see through it, but not the immature.* [170–171]

LIKE A MIRAGE in the desert or froth on the seashore, the body will fade away. Open any family album; you will see that the life it captures really does look like a mirage. You will see some member of the older generation, perhaps a beloved aunt, as a little girl playing on a tricycle, then as an attractive young woman going to a dance or behind the wheel of a new car. Then, as you turn the pages, there she is getting married, having children, and before your eyes she slowly acquires the serene beauty of the middle-aged woman you know.

How can a mirage bring security? The Buddha does not say that security is impossible, but he reminds us, again and again, that we cannot draw security from the body, or anything else in the world of change.

*All created things are transitory; those who
realize this are freed from suffering. This is the
path that leads to pure wisdom.* [277]

ON THE NIGHT of his awakening, the Buddha saw with the eye of illumination that all existence is impermanent – a process which continues without a break, constantly renewing itself. It is due to our abysmal ignorance and our tempestuous passions that things seem to have permanence and identity.

Because all things are impermanent they can never be a source of happiness to us. They can never be a source of support or consolation. When, however, we obtain a deep insight into the true nature of things, we become free – completely, ultimately, and abidingly free from all selfish craving, which is the cause of our suffering.

Therefore, it is in order to liberate us that the Buddha brings home to us the nature of his vision of impermanence, using an analytical approach that is at once simple and profound. He says we are made up of five *skandhas* or "heaps," all subject to change: form, sensation, perception, mental formations, and consciousness. The first of these pertains to the body, and the other four to the mind. Just as the body is constantly changing, the mind as well is a field of forces in constant flux. In short, the human individual is a combination of changing physical and mental elements.

In this sense, the Buddha would say, "There is no such person as Jim. There is only an ever-changing combination of physical and mental energies which for the sake of convenience we call Jim."

My village in Kerala, like all Indian villages, sets aside one day of the week as market day, when all the small farmers around come with vegetables, fruits, and spices to sell. They sit by the roadside, where they spread a big jute cloth on which to display their wares. One or two sellers will always have colorful heaps of spices – yellow, red, black, white, and green. These are the turmeric, red pepper, black mustard seed, fenugreek, ginger, and coriander essential in almost every Indian dish.

A customer comes and says, "I am going to prepare dinner and I've got a certain menu, so I need five of your spices." The seller takes a big banana leaf and twists it into a container. Then she takes one scoop from the heap of coriander, one from the fenugreek, one from the ginger, one from the mustard seed, and finally one little pinch from the chilies. She ties the bundle up with a string, smiling and saying, "Now you can take it home and prepare your dinner."

The Buddha uses this village image to say that each of us is made up of a packet of ingredients like spices, each chosen and mixed up in order to cook a particular curry.

The first heap is simply form. To make a human being, first you take a pinch from the heap called form, which is the body. The second heap, sensation, is more subtle, but it's still fairly easy to recognize: it is the simple mental event that takes place when the senses come in contact with a sense object. Third is perception – or, more accurately, naming, classification – which is another kind of mental event. Ideas, thoughts, and abstractions are all from the heap called perception, and they are essential to the mix. Otherwise, what would we talk about? How would we communicate?

The fourth ingredient is more subtle still – in fact, its very presence is not acknowledged most of the time, unless we have undergone a certain period of meditation and spiritual discipline. But it is there, operating day in and day out in the human personality. This heap consists of what the Buddha calls *samskaras* – a word that is usually translated as "mental formations," though I prefer to use the Sanskrit word because it is more precise. Like the body, sensations, and perceptions, samskaras are subject to change. Every day, every moment, we are creating samskaras, bit by bit, and at the same time we are dismantling them bit by bit, to build new samskaras. This is one of the most promising of the Buddha's teachings: our samskaras, our tendencies, can change, *must* change. It was an astounding discovery for me when I began to understand what samskaras are, how they are formed, and how they can be changed, because I understood that personality itself can be changed.

Finally we come to the last pinch of spice, which is usually translated as consciousness. I find it more helpful to say separate consciousness or individual consciousness, I-consciousness – it's right at the top of the parcel, the crowning touch.

So there we have the five ingredients that make up the human creature, and they are all subject to change, which is the point of the Buddha's analysis: "Form is foam; sensations are bubbles; perception is a mirage. Samskaras are like the trunk of the plantain tree; consciousness is but an illusion."

The Buddha is not trying to please us or displease us with this analysis. He is not criticizing human nature or running us down. He is simply telling us what life is like. Everything is changing; everything is made up of components that come into being and then pass away – even the human personality, even who we are.

In the second century B.C., an Indo-Greek king named

Milinda – called Menander in the Greek chronicles – ruled over a large kingdom extending from Afghanistan into Northern India. Milinda loved to debate questions of philosophy, and he had a reputation for trying to beat others in argument. But he was also a sincere seeker who could ask practical questions. When he heard that a wise monk named Nagasena, a devoted follower of the Buddha, was traveling through his lands, Milinda was eager to pay him a visit.

Now Nagasena had heard about how King Milinda loved to debate and argue, but he told his fellow monks, "Let him come. Have no fear! Even if all the kings of India were to come, we would meet them with answers to their questions."

Soon Milinda found out where the monk was staying and went to see him, accompanied by his large Greek retinue. The Venerable Nagasena and his monks received the king warmly, and after the greetings and courtesies were over, Milinda asked the sage, "What is your reverence's name?"

The sage replied, "I am known as Nagasena, gracious king, and that is how everyone addresses me. But though I am known as Nagasena, that is only a designation, an appellation, a mere name. For there is no real person who has the name Nagasena."

Enjoying the contest of wits, the king declared, "Listen, you Greeks and monks! This Nagasena says he is not a real person! How can I be expected to agree with that? I ask you, Venerable Nagasena, if no person exists, then who receives the robes, food, and lodging that your students offer you? Who follows morality, practices meditation, and attains nirvana? Then surely there is a 'Nagasena'? Perhaps the hairs on your head are 'Nagasena'?"

The poker-faced monk replied, "No, great king!"

"Perhaps the nails, teeth, skin, muscles?"

"No, great king."

"Perhaps the feeling, perceptions, mental formations, or consciousness are Nagasena?"

"No, great king."

"Then I can discover no Nagasena at all," Milinda exclaimed. "'Nagasena' is just a mere sound."

Thereupon Nagasena smiled and asked, "How did you come here, your majesty, on foot or in a chariot?"

"I did not come on foot, sir, but in a chariot."

"If you have come in a chariot, please explain to me what a chariot is. Is it the axle? Or the wheels, or the chassis, or reins, or yoke that is the chariot?"

"No, reverend sir! It is none of these."

"Is it all of these combined, or is it something apart from them?"

"No, reverend sir!"

"Then, ask as I may, I can discover no chariot at all," Nagasena replied. "Your majesty has spoken a falsehood! Now listen, you Greeks and monks, this King Milinda tells me that he has come in a chariot. But when asked to show me the chariot, he cannot. How can I approve of that?"

The Greeks applauded the Venerable Nagasena and said to Milinda, "Let your majesty get out of that if you can!"

But King Milinda said to Nagasena, "I have not spoken a falsehood." Then he pondered, inspecting the chariot and weighing his answer carefully. "It is in dependence . . . on the wheels . . . the chassis . . . the reins . . . the yoke . . . the pole . . . the axle . . . that there is this designation 'chariot.'"

"Your majesty has spoken well about the chariot! Just so with me. In dependence on the five skandhas there takes place this denomination 'Nagasena.' In ultimate reality, however, this person cannot be apprehended," the monk explained. "Where all constituent parts are present, the word 'chariot' is applied. So likewise where the skandhas are, the term 'a being' commonly is used."

"Wonderful, Nagasena! That is astonishing!"

Then all the Greeks applauded, with Milinda leading.

"Most brilliantly have these questions been answered. Were the Buddha himself here, he would approve all you have said. Well spoken, Nagasena, well spoken!"

Yes, there is a process called "Nagasena" – but in the ultimate sense, there is no Nagasena to be found. He is not a person but a process, not a noun but a verb. He is . . . impermanent. Step by step the Buddha has pushed us into a corner. His logic cannot be denied.

All states are without self; those who realize
this are freed from suffering. This is the path
that leads to pure wisdom. [279]

NAGASENA IS A process, according to the Buddha, and that process is literally *anatta, an-atma,* "without a self" – which is not easy to understand. Like King Milinda, we want to protest that of course there is a "self" or "person" that is Nagasena. It is easy to see why there has been so much controversy over what the Buddha meant. Did he teach a belief in an immortal self beyond the mortal, personal ego, as the scriptures of the Vedic tradition do, or did he teach that there is no immortal self? One way to answer this controversy is to say that when we practice the Buddha's teachings instead of dealing with them intellectually, we will begin to understand what he means by "not-self." In other words, this is not an intellectual question, so it cannot be answered by intellectual argument.

The important thing to understand is that in describing the skandhas, the Buddha strikes us a hard blow: the birth of any individual person – Nagasena, for example – is the coming together of the skandhas, and the death of the individual person is the breaking apart of these same skandhas – without reference to an individual self or soul. The personal ego, which seems so real and considers its satisfactions so all-important, is just a bundle of thoughts, memories, desires, fears, urges, anxieties, and aspirations that is largely an illusion – a flux of separate mental events temporarily associated with a physical body, but nothing that anyone could call a whole. The teaching of the skandhas is a way, a method, to break down our attachment – our clinging – to the body and all the rest.

The Buddha says, "This body is without a self." If we look carefully, we see that he says, "This *body* is without a self." I would put it practically by saying that this body is the jacket I wear, the car I drive, the house in which I live. It is not my self. Even if you are a perfect driver and can establish rapport with your car, you know you are not your car. You know you are not the clothes you wear or the house in which you live. Similarly, the Buddha says, you are not your body.

To further convince us, the Buddha adds, "If this body were the Self, it would not be involved in sickness and old age. But one cannot command the body and say, 'Let my body be healthy. Let my body not be unhealthy.'" This is how the Buddha drives us into a corner with his ruthless reasoning. If the body were me, then I would be able to tell it to be well and it would be well. I would be able to tell it not to die and it would not die.

Then, being a careful teacher, the Buddha persists through all the skandhas: "So also with regard to feelings, perceptions, samskaras, and consciousness. Each is not the Self. This is not me. This am I not. This is not the Self."

I can imagine the Buddha as a lecturer, standing in front of his big blackboard as he drives his point home. "Now what do you think, Class, is the body permanent or impermanent?"

The students, being as careful as the teacher, think for a long time, and perhaps even discuss it amongst themselves. Finally they say, "Impermanent, sir!"

"And is what is impermanent good or bad?"

The disciples of the Buddha heave a sigh. "Bad, sir!"

"Then when it comes to what is impermanent and sorrowful, is it fitting to say, 'This is me. I am this. This is my Self'?"

They all look down and groan, "Surely not!"

So also is it with feeling, perception, mental formations, and consciousness. They are all impermanent. They are not the Self.

MY LIFE, YOUR life, is changing from instant to instant. You are not the same person you were when you lived in Los Angeles, yet you are not another. When you come back from Mexico or Costa Rica you will not be the same, nor will you be another. The Buddha puts it most concisely: "He is not the same, yet he is not someone else." There is great hope in this little statement, because it means that change for the better is possible. If a person is a process, that process can be changed, directed, even reversed.

"She is not the same, yet she is not another." There is a blessing hidden in this. If I'm not the same person today as I was yesterday, I can forgive the mistakes I made in my ignorance yesterday and live more wisely today. I can forgive and forget and move on. This is the hopeful teaching of the Buddha: we are not programmed by our genes, our past, or fate. Because we will not be the same person tomorrow, transformation is possible.

The approach of traditional Indian philosophy is perhaps easier to understand. Indian philosophy agrees that there is a small self composed of skandhas that is unreal, but also that there is a higher Self called the *Atman,* and the discovery of this Self is the goal of all spiritual disciplines. In this Hindu approach we are told that if we can divest ourselves of all negative tendencies, what is left is positive; if we can divest ourselves from a false identification with body and mind, what is left is pure spirit. In the Buddha's teaching, the emphasis is more on "not this, not this": I am not my body, not my thoughts, not my samskaras. But whether we use the language of Self or not-self, the important thing is to overcome the belief in a false self that can be fulfilled separate from the whole.

When all that we are not has been eliminated, what remains is nirvana. Nirvana cannot be described; the experience of not-self cannot be described. Sometimes peculiar statements are made about what these mean when writers and philosophers try to describe a condition which is beyond subject and object, knower and known. This is where the Buddha adopted a practical outlook: if you want to know nirvana there is only one way, and that is for you to find out for yourself. There is no other way.

Rather than argue about what nirvana is and what it is not, the Buddha says, "Get in the boat! Start the journey. You will find for yourself what is beyond the world of change and suffering."

> *Take refuge in the Buddha, the dharma, and*
> *the sangha and you will grasp the Four Noble*
> *Truths: suffering, the cause of suffering, the end*
> *of suffering, and the Noble Eightfold Path that*
> *takes you beyond suffering. That is your best*
> *refuge, your only refuge. When you reach it, all*
> *sorrow falls away.* [190–192]

"I TEACH THE end of suffering." This is perhaps the most profound statement in all of Buddhist literature. The Buddha's analysis of our human suffering, apart from all his other teachings, makes him an extraordinary spiritual genius and a superb physician of the mind.

After he attained his awakening, the Buddha went to Sarnath, near Benares, the ancient city on the River Ganges. There at the Deer Park he delivered his first sermon, "Setting the Wheel of the Dharma in Motion." The text of this first sermon contains the Four Noble Truths that explain what keeps us on this shore of change and suffering.

The First Noble Truth is that life is *duhkha*, or sorrow. Birth is sorrow, disease is sorrow, decay is sorrow, death is sorrow. When the Buddha says that life is sorrow, he is not being pessimistic. The word *duhkha* has the connotation of something being off – for example, of an axle being off center in a wheel, or of a bone being out of joint. The meaning of the First Noble

Truth is that something is radically wrong with life as it is usually lived.

The Second Noble Truth brings out the cause of the malady: *trishna,* "thirst," which is called *tanha* in Pali. Naturally, if we can eliminate the cause, we can eliminate the disease – and when the disease is cured, all of us can attain nirvana. This thirst consists of all self-centered desires, which we are prepared to satisfy if necessary at the cost of others. The cause of our illness is not desire; it is *selfish* desire that the Buddha calls thirst.

The Third Noble Truth follows logically from the second. If the cause of suffering is the craving for private, personal satisfaction, then the cure lies in the conquest of such cravings. If we could only break out of the prison-house of separateness into the universal expanse of cosmic life, there would immediately be an end to our suffering – an end to duhkha. Therefore, far from being fatalistic or life-denying, the Buddha is offering compelling hope and confidence.

The Buddhist sutras tell us that King Bimbisara, the ruler of Magadha in those days, learned this truth about life from the Buddha himself. One day, King Bimbisara, who was deeply devoted to the Buddha, approached the Blessed One in the beautiful grove where he was spending the rainy season. As soon as the courtesies had been exchanged, the king asked the question we all ask at one time or another: "Why am I unhappy?"

The Blessed One, always appealing to reason, begins to speak. "It is not because you do not have money that you are unhappy. It is not because you lack fame. You are unhappy and you will continue to be unhappy no matter how rich or famous you are, as long as you have selfish desires. If you can overcome those selfish desires, you will live in abiding joy, which is nirvana. Sire, I can show you the path by which you can get rid of these selfish desires."

Such was the power of the message – so direct, so simple, so personal – that King Bimbisara became a disciple of the Buddha.

After diagnosing our problem, in the Fourth Noble Truth the Buddha gives us not a philosophy but a method to bring an end to our suffering: the Noble Eightfold Path. He is not asking us to lead a life of self-abnegation, as an end to selfish desire might imply. He gives us what he called the Middle Path, neither self-indulgence nor self-denial. It is Right Understanding, Right Purpose, Right Speech, Right Action, Right Occupation, Right Effort, Right Attention, and Right Meditation.

> *There is no gift better than the gift of the*
> *dharma, no gift more sweet, no gift more joyful.*
> *It puts an end to cravings and the sorrow they*
> *bring.* [354]

RIGHT UNDERSTANDING IS the very first point of the Buddha's Eightfold Path, because as long as we do not understand life as it really is, we will make demands which life cannot fulfill. Then we become unhappy, frustrated, and bitter, and go about nursing grievances against others. It is because we do not know anything about the nature of life that we make foolish, selfish demands.

For example, we demand that nothing change. As we pass from our twenties to thirties, we try to cling to the twenties. We feel pleased when a friend says, "You don't look a day over twenty," even if we are ten years older. In a small way we are making an impossible demand on life: May I always be twenty.

This is understandable. It is natural to try to cling to youth and think "I never want to change." But that is not the way life is. Right Understanding is to know that change is the nature of life and real beauty is not limited by age.

Take another example of wrong understanding which leads us to make another kind of demand on life: the demand that acquiring material possessions makes us happy. We go on accumulating things, buying things, in the hope that this will bring us happiness, but according to the Buddha, these things are impermanent; they come and go. Therefore they can never make us happy.

The secret of duhkha and the overcoming of duhkha is profoundly simple: as long as we wander in search of satisfactions outside, we will remain unfulfilled. It may be a thirst for little things – dinner at a restaurant, a movie, a shopping trip – or it may be something bigger, such as wealth, power, or fame. Whatever it is, as long as the drive is selfish, we are wandering outside, and so we will always be insecure, always be unsatisfied.

As long as our happiness is dependent upon fulfilling some condition outside – as long as there is an "if" anywhere – the Buddha's truth about suffering will rule our lives. But as we begin to bring back all our selfish desires and unite them into the supreme desire for nirvana, gradually we will find sorrow leaving us.

FOR MANY OF us, the other shore beckons, but we wonder if we have the capacity to reach it. We feel we may not have the dedication and determination to make this crossing. To such people, the Buddha says that no one need feel inadequate to the demands of this adventure. It is difficult, no one would deny that, but the Buddha is always at our side, showing us the way and healing our wounds with his little first-aid kit.

Particularly for those who are intellectually oriented, as most of us in the modern world are, it is natural to have doubts about the reality of nirvana and our capacity to reach it. It is natural to ask, "What's this talk about nirvana? This is all right for a course in philosophy, but isn't it absurd to practice these Buddhist disciplines in the expectation that there is a supreme goal?" This question was asked during the time of the Buddha, and it has been asked in every age since. But the Buddha does not try to justify himself. He simply says, "Come and see." His wisdom and compassion are proof that this is a desirable way of life. That's what every intelligent observer absorbs.

Perhaps, for many, even when the goal beckons, we find our commitment may not go deep enough. There is nothing wrong with us, the Buddha assures us; we simply need to deepen our commitment to reach the goal. If we can learn how to put more energy into our desire to cross the river – if we can drive that desire deeper and make the commitment stronger – our progress will be sure and swift.

I had no extraordinary gifts when I started the spiritual life, but through my teacher's blessing and guidance, I gradually learned the art of unifying my desires in order to make my desire for nirvana overwhelming. I learned the most precious, the most practical, and the most difficult skill on earth, which is how to channel my desires. It is a strange art, a strange alchemy, where you find, say, a desire for money or a desire for possessions and transform those desires into an overwhelming desire to go deeper in meditation.

Many, many people have confided in me that they fear they don't have the energy, the drive, to practice the spiritual disciplines necessary for making this journey. I have been able to help them by showing them how to recall their desires from wasteful channels to add to their drive and add to their capacity to complete the journey. I tell them about the dynamics of desire – not about right or wrong, or even about moral or immoral. Drawing on years of experience, I tell them that they have abundant energy, but it is not under their control. They have a lot of drive, but it is frittered away through many channels, some of which may look completely safe. Even a little desire has tremendous power packed in it.

Every one of us doubts our ability to make the journey. Yes, we agree, life would be better without selfish desire and suffering, but how can anyone overcome these? When the Buddha says we can free ourselves from suffering by conquering our selfish desires, we naturally think it's impossible. Our desires appear so large, so outsized, that we may simply accept that they can never be defeated. Actually, if we examine them closely, we will see that nearly all of these desires are rather weak, even puny. It's our constant dwelling on them that makes them flourish. "Oh, I wish I could have that. I wish I could be with her." Bit by bit, this constant, unremitting craving transforms what was a tentative desire into a monster. But this process is not inevitable.

We do have some ability to direct our desires, and we can increase that capacity through spiritual disciplines – until we are the owners of our passions, and therefore of our lives.

> *Better than ruling this world, better than*
> *attaining the realm of the gods, better than*
> *being lord of all the worlds, is one step taken*
> *on the path to nirvana.* [178]

IT IS NOT difficult to understand that in life we must have a direction, a higher goal. If we haven't found it, there will always be an emptiness in our heart. We can go round the world, we can attend parties in London and Moscow, we can climb mountains or sail over oceans, but inside there will always be this haunting insecurity. We can read a library of books, we can create works of art, we can have a large bank account, but without an overriding goal life deteriorates into utter boredom, which is the source of great misery.

For the Buddha, this supreme goal is nirvana. If I can harness my deepest urges in this magnificent endeavor to achieve nirvana, I come to life. If I try to live for myself, I wither away and die. But as long as I keep my eyes on this supreme goal, my life will be a great adventure.

When I have a supreme goal, even if I find a detour or a blind alley alluring, instead of being drawn to that I can keep my eyes on my goal and draw myself away from the temptation. For those who do not have an overriding goal, there is no incentive, no motivation, to resist the blandishments of egocentric life.

Every one of us has the capacity to conquer the infinite. This is the deepest longing which all of us carry through many lives. Hence, eventually we will tire of every achievement that is finite. This is the glory of human nature: for us there is no joy in the finite; there is joy only in the infinite.

> *The earnest spiritual aspirant, fearing sloth,*
> *advances like a fire, burning all fetters. Such*
> *seekers will never fall back: they are nearing*
> *nirvana.* [31–32]
>
> *Wake up! Don't be lazy. Follow the right path,*
> *avoid the wrong. You will be happy here as*
> *well as hereafter.* [168–169]

THE BUDDHA BECKONS to us with more and more persistence: *Find your courage! Kindle your enthusiasm!* Don't postpone the spiritual journey, no matter what obstacles seem to stand in the way. This is the urgent message of the Buddha. All kinds of plausible excuses can always be found. Our tooth is aching, so we must go to the dentist and get it set right. After that there is a stomach problem. Even if there are no physical problems, there is emotional stress. If we are going to postpone until the body is completely healthy and our mind at peace, the journey will be delayed for a long, long time.

All of us have difficulties, both physical and mental, but the Buddha assures us that we can begin this journey with all our problems. What guide in the world will accept us and welcome us if we show up with a backpack full of problems? Imagine arriving at the point of departure only to have your guide ask, "What are all these bags?"

"These are my problems," you say, "Can I bring them along?"

Any guide worth his salt will say, "You'd better find some other companion."

But when the Buddha looks at all the bags, he says, "May I carry some of them for you? Give me the heavier ones." Then he will add, "This journey is meant for people with problems."

Wake up! Seek the highest! The stubborn call will not leave us in peace. For when the appearance of change and separateness vanishes, nirvana remains. Seek nirvana here and now because it is the highest joy. It is security, the absence of fear, peace of mind, freedom from compulsions and illness. It is untouched by age and unaffected by death. Those who find refuge in the island of nirvana live in the sea of change without being swept away. They know what life is, and they know there is something more. Lacking nothing, craving nothing, they stay in the world solely to help and serve. We cannot say they live without grief; it is their sensitiveness to the suffering of others that motivates their lives. But personal sorrow is gone. They live to give, and their capacity to go on giving is a source of joy so great that it cannot be measured against any reward the world can offer.

or wealth or learning who will reach the goal. It's the person with continuing enthusiasm – morning, noon, and night.

Sustained enthusiasm is a precious quality with a power that cold logic does not have. In any walk of life we can see that the most effective person is not one who is merely learned or the one who has the most experience, but the one who is on fire. It's the teacher with enthusiasm who can reach her students, the doctor with a passion to heal who often succeeds where others fail.

My little niece once teased me that my initials E.E. stand for "extreme enthusiasm," and if I can claim any exceptional quality, it would be enthusiasm, which was an early characteristic of mine. If I experienced something, I had to share it. When I was starting out as a professor of English literature, there were many better scholars than I was – it was my gusto for Shakespeare and Shaw and Wordsworth that appealed to my students.

The person who lacks enthusiasm lacks everything, but the person who has enthusiasm can harness that passion to reach his or her goal, including the goal of nirvana. Most important of all, enthusiasm in and of itself brings joy. Just as a hiker begins with an eagerness to hit the trail, so does the seeker for nirvana welcome the journey. Nirvana is limitless joy, limitless security. If you are on the road to limitless joy and limitless security, right from the outset shouldn't you have the joy of sincere enthusiasm? This does not mean somber determination – "Even if it kills me, I am going to achieve nirvana!" It is just the opposite. The goal may be far, far distant. We may not even have a glimpse of the final destination. But we know we are on the road, and this knowledge gives us joy.

No matter how strong our dedication, however, we should not undertake this journey under the impression that it can be made in one quick dash. We should be prepared for a long, difficult crossing, and without earnestness we cannot sustain the journey. When put into everyday language, this means we keep our eyes focused always on the goal, and refrain from doing anything that impedes us while taking care to do everything that helps us. The secret is not to think in terms of everlasting vigilance, from this day forward, but of this moment. Think in terms of moment-by-moment enthusiasm, and never lack in earnestness.

Over and over again, the Buddha tells us we can all make the journey to nirvana – not by colossal steps, not instantaneously, but little by little, every day, both during meditation and during our daily routine – at work, in the store, in the kitchen, at school, in the home. It's done slowly, gently, by taming the whims and caprices of the mind.

> *Earnest among those who are indolent, awake*
> *among those who slumber, the wise advance*
> *like a racehorse, leaving others behind. It was*
> *through earnest effort that Indra became lord*
> *of the gods. The earnest are always respected,*
> *the indolent never.* [29–30]

WHEN I HAD started the practice of meditation and made it the foundation of my life, self-doubt would still sometimes upset my mind. I wanted to meet the challenges facing me, yet my old conditioning was a big obstacle. My mind would play a clever card: "You won't be able to meet the challenge." This is common in the early days, and most of us will have to undergo these doubts.

As I began to throw my weight more and more on the spiritual side of the argument, a wonderful transformation came about. One day, instead of feeling inadequate, I realized I was ready to meet the challenge. It was a very encouraging discovery. Formerly, when temptations or difficulties would come, I would think, "Wouldn't I like to yield?" I would feel it was going to be too difficult to resist. But now, instead of feeling inadequate, to my surprise the mental state was: I am adequate. The temptations were still there, the difficulties were still there, but my belief in myself had changed. Once I reached this state, I was confident that even if it took time I could overcome all those temptations. I could meet the challenge.

For all of us this self-belief changes gradually, due to hard work and continuing vigilance and enthusiasm. With every step forward, you gain in understanding and earnestness. Then you can take the next step. With each step, your security grows; you feel a new energy.

The progress may seem agonizingly slow, but it is genuine, and its very slowness will protect us from harm. Some have such an all-consuming desire to cross the river of life and attain nirvana that they may be tempted to force change, and even do violence to themselves through a misguided effort. The scriptures warn us many times that there is no genuine spiritual progress to be found in drugs or in running away from life or in any other violent method. When the Buddhist sutras tell us how many lifetimes the Buddha-to-be practiced spiritual disciplines, it is to show that these changes cannot come about quickly.

Time and gentleness are required. Yet those who keep their eyes focused always on the supreme goal, refraining from doing anything that impedes them and taking care to do everything that helps them, will find their progress is remarkable.

> *Raise yourself by your own efforts; be your own*
> *critic. Thus self-reliant and vigilant, you will*
> *live in joy. Be your own master and protector.*
> *Train your mind as a merchant trains his horse.*
> [379–380]

TRAINING THE MIND requires constant effort, continuing enthusiasm, often in spite of difficulties and disappointments. Training the body is easier to understand, because it comes more naturally. For example, most of us are more vigilant about diet and exercise than we are about harmful mental states like anger. Most of us are eager to exercise because we understand that it is good for the body to walk, run, and swim. If we don't get our quota of exercise every week, we feel deprived. But the Buddha would say that even if we have put in the necessary hours of running and walking, if we have let the mind flounder in unkindness and impatience we have failed to train properly.

Most of us have learned to be scrupulous about the body. A slight cut on the finger means we apply a Band-Aid and keep it from getting wet. We'll ask the doctor if we need a tetanus shot and we will worry about infection, all because there is a cut on the hand. The Buddha says yes, we should care for the body, but why not guard the mind with equal care? If an impatient thought arises, there is likely to be infection of our mood. If a resentment is nursed, there can be much worse consequences than a little wound on the finger. Because we are physically oriented, we say, "Oh, resentments can cure themselves. Just give them a little time." The Buddha understands that we aren't prepared to take these mental states seriously, so he cautions us to guard the mind very carefully.

> *Guard yourself well, both within and without,*
> *like a well-defended fort. Don't waste a*
> *moment, for wasted moments send you on the*
> *downward course.* [315]

IN INDIA IT is not uncommon to see traces of a medieval town right in the middle of a bustling modern city. Early in my teaching career at a college in Central India, I remember visiting the nearby town where I could still see the two gates that guarded the city in past centuries. In medieval times, sentries checked on anyone who was coming in. Anyone who was likely to cause a disturbance would not be admitted.

Similarly, the Buddha says, "Don't let just any thoughts come into your mind." They should be checked by the security people at the gate. If the thought is likely to disturb your mind, keep the thought out. If the thought is beneficial, welcome it and say, "I am glad to have you. Make yourself at home." It is this capacity to exclude disruptive thoughts and to admit helpful thoughts that is at the very core of vigilance.

Most of us may have never seen a fort, never tried to gain entry to one, but we've all seen a big queue outside a theater with people impatient to get in. Someone is always there to check tickets. Otherwise, some unruly fellows will just barge in and say, "Come on, everybody! The door is open." The crowd goes in and occupies the theater. That's what happens when our mind is untrained and we lack vigilance. In a moment, a crowd of thoughts enters, all clamoring for our attention.

Without some training of the mind, without some mastery over our attention, any compulsive thought can just walk in and take over. We can get caught even in little things which appeal to us because they give us pleasure or tickle our vanity. We get caught in work that we like, people that we like, food that we like, without asking how beneficial they are.

> *It is hard to leave the world and hard to live in it, painful to live with the worldly and painful to be a wanderer. Reach the goal; you will wander and suffer no more.* [302]

TODAY IN BERKELEY I saw a large truck with a sign at the back: Frequent Stops. There are a lot of people who can have this sign on their back. They have to go to this restaurant to taste some gourmet dish, then go to the jewelry store, then walk across to an old bookshop to pick up some curious volume. Millions of human beings go through life like this. As long as they are pulled by pleasure and profit, this is how life is: frequent stops.

Yet there is a rare type who can carry that other message we see on the Bay Bridge: No Stopping, No Turning. This is the person, seldom found in any country, who makes straight for the goal. Let there be many distractions, let there be many temptations; often they do not even see them. Even if they do see them, it has no effect on them because their eyes are completely on the goal. The Buddha says such people will reach nirvana, because they are not going to allow themselves to be distracted.

> *As rain seeps through an ill-thatched hut,*
> *passion will seep through an untrained mind.*
>
> *As rain cannot seep through a well-thatched*
> *hut, passion cannot seep through a well-*
> *trained mind.* [13–14]

VIGILANCE WHERE THE mind is concerned is one of the Buddha's favorite subjects. On this subject he is unyielding, because he knows the mind is just waiting for the day when you are careless so it can do what it likes. I have friendly relations with my body – I like to call it my "buddy" – but when it comes to the mind, I keep a close eye on it. I won't easily trust the mind because I know how clever it is. I can make a concession to the body now and then, on a special occasion, but as far as the mind is concerned, the Buddha says, don't ever lose your vigilance. Be polite, be courteous, but don't be lax.

Sometimes we may fall into the comforting notion that because we have resolved to meditate and follow the way of the Buddha we are not going to face temptations. It's a comforting thought, but unfortunately it is not likely to be true. In fact, right from the outset there is trouble. Somehow, just when you are getting interested in what the Buddha has to teach, somebody promises you a ticket to the Shakespearian festival in Stratford-on-Avon, along with the airplane ticket you need to attend.

There have been many, many good aspirants who say, "Oh, after I come back from the Shakespeare festival I am really going to get serious." They attend the festival, get interested in a particular actress, and hang about the theater even when all the plays have closed. Ultimately, they follow her back to London and are given a small role as an extra carrying a sword. This is how even the most vigilant get entangled. Even a little temptation can gradually become huge once you get entangled. It's the old story of getting compulsively sucked in.

For someone else it may be a global tour. "Just let me finish my travels. I want to go round the world because I have never been away from home." She goes round the world and in Hong Kong she finds such bargains that she buys a lot of things, takes them back to San Francisco, and sets up a store. After a while she is so successful that she opens another store in Palo Alto, then in Seattle, then in Boston. Eventually she is the ruler of a vast commercial enterprise. This kind of thing has happened to more than a few who wanted to follow the spiritual life.

Again we can find an illustration in a story about Bimbisara, who was a good ruler but who had been brought up in the royal tradition of using force against those whom he considered his enemies. On the positive side, King Bimbisara was a sensitive, well-intentioned man who tried to rule his kingdom with sympathy for his people, but on the negative side he could resort to violent means.

Bimbisara was familiar with the Buddha's family and knew the Buddha's father, so when he met Siddhartha when he was on his way to the forest, the king tried to prevent the young prince from renouncing the world to seek a spiritual fortune. Struck by the regal majesty of young Siddhartha, Bimbisara said, "You'll make a great king, Siddhartha. Why do you want to go to the forest? Don't go, and I'll share my kingdom with you."

The Buddha does not argue, does not try to defend himself. He smiles, wishes his majesty well, and continues on. No wasting words, no stopping – that's the Buddha.

> *If you meditate earnestly, pure in mind and*
> *kind in deeds, leading a disciplined life in*
> *harmony with the dharma, you will grow in*
> *glory.* [24]

BE VIGILANT, THE Buddha says. Don't let the mind wander aimlessly. Again the Buddha's counsel is so simple, so concise, that we may miss the wealth of practical wisdom it contains. When we let our attention wander, most of us will find that we begin to suffer emotional problems. To let our attention wander is inviting trouble. Therefore, the training of attention must be continued throughout the day. In the morning period of meditation we keep the mind firmly in hand, but after we get up from meditation we can't afford to say, "Okay, mind, you can jump over the fence now and run away."

Whatever we do with concentration helps to train the mind. In the office, at the clinic, at the store, at school, wherever we are working, we are also training the mind. Over a long period, this is the wonderful development: one-pointed attention becomes natural. There is no effort; there is no tension. This kind of natural one-pointed attention gives us a wonderful confidence that we can bring all our resources to bear upon a problem. We don't get insecure when we know we can bring together all our faculties to meet a challenge.

There is a close connection between concentration and enthusiasm. If we find we cannot finish what we have taken up, the reason may be a short span of attention. Our ability to concentrate is weak. Even if we have enthusiasm, we work for half an hour with gusto and then our will collapses. At that time, it is possible to resist the wave of lassitude and give our attention more and more to the task. To our surprise we will find that our enthusiasm for the task has suddenly returned.

Those with scientific or artistic talent are often capable of long periods of concentration, but this is not necessarily an inborn trait. The capacity to concentrate for long periods can be cultivated by all of us by not giving in when we feel a little tired or a little bored. These are tricks of the mind when it doesn't want to be brought under control. Practicing one-pointed concentration in everything we do is a great aid in transforming carelessness into earnestness.

Then again, when concentration is good, we must make sure it isn't compulsive. In compulsive concentration we can do tremendous things, but unfortunately they may not be beneficial. Concentration is effective when it is free, when we can direct it at will, but concentration can lead to disaster when it is obsessive. In all obsessions, as the victims can testify, there is imprisoned concentration. We just cannot shake it off. The Old Man of the Sea sits on our shoulders, pressing harder and harder, and we cannot escape. We are caught in a narrow compulsion and we cannot remember the whole picture, which means we have lost the ability to make a beneficial contribution.

This can even become a grave threat to our own welfare and the welfare of others.

When our concentration is not under our control, we will find that enthusiasm comes and goes, waxes and wanes. The deadline is looming and we put up a little placard in our office or studio, "Beat the Deadline! March 31!" But in spite of the best intentions, we just can't bring ourselves to sit down, open the book, and get out the papers.

Whenever we find we must do something we don't particularly like – a job, a project, an important letter – suddenly we find that energy has just withdrawn from our arm. We don't know what happened. It's not our fault, surely, but our arms have suddenly grown numb. We cannot wash the dishes. We cannot lift the pots and pans. Some mysterious deflating process has struck us down. We're all familiar with this feeling – but it's not in the body; it's in the mind.

Our enthusiasm for the job has simply vanished, and, curiously, we suddenly find some other job to attend to – usually something not essential. On these occasions, it is not lack of energy or enterprise or stamina that thwarts us. We just don't know how to direct our enthusiasm. There is energy, but it is not under our control.

Imagine there is a fire, and the fire engine arrives with sirens blaring. The firefighters jump off the truck and run to the blaze, but instead of directing the hose on the fire they aim at the assembled crowd. Everyone shouts, "We're not on fire! The *house* is on fire!" The firefighters say, "We don't know how to direct the hose, so we are dousing you."

In my many years as a college professor, I found that with

most students a simple tip was helpful. I'd say, first, go directly to your desk and sit down in your chair. Second, take out your work and pretend that you are doing it. Just go through the motions. You are just pretending to take your book to open it to section two. Then, third, pretend to start writing. If you keep pretending for a page or two – keep writing, keep studying – soon you'll be engrossed in the task. Once you are absorbed, you may not even know that it's dinnertime. Someone will have to come and remind you.

This proves that lack of energy is not the problem. Somehow we have to trick the mind, which is reluctant to settle down. The monkey mind plays many tricks on us every day, so isn't it fair to play a trick on the mind now and then?

When our enthusiasm fails, it is sometimes masked as the issue of boredom. The job is boring, our studies are boring, our relationships are boring. And sometimes they can be. When a job bores us, our response is to lose interest in it and do it half-heartedly. We don't realize we can dispel the boredom by giving the task more attention. The moment we attend to any job completely, it becomes all-absorbing. It is our inability to give our attention to the work at hand that makes it monotonous. The Buddha says whatever you do, do it with all your attention, all your concentration: "When you walk, walk. When you sit, sit. Don't wobble." If we can do this, we are not likely to be bored.

These are simple hints to help us kindle our enthusiasm. For some, a regular schedule is a great aid if it can be observed carefully. For others, it helps considerably to have a visible reminder that there are certain jobs to be done. Some find it helpful to have a little note over the washbasin: "If you don't like doing something, now is the time to do it." That is a dramatic way to bring enthusiasm to life, one that appeals to me very much.

Most of the time, the mind just repeats its favorite line over and over: "I don't want to do this. I don't want to do that." And most of the time the mind gets its way. Nonetheless there is a keen joy in defying the mind by saying, "I am going to do it even if you don't like it!" These are some of the creative games we can play with the mind, which is always playing games with us. Whenever you find that you dislike something important, try to do it immediately. By these simple disciplines we can go a long, long way in transforming indifference into earnestness.

> *Be vigilant; guard your mind against negative*
> *thoughts. Pull yourself out of bad ways as an*
> *elephant raises itself out of the mud.* [327]

THE PERSON WHO succeeds is the one who is vigilant on little occasions as well as large. On major occasions most people are on their guard, but on little occasions it is easy to forget. Students of literature may be familiar with a book by G. K. Chesterton called *Tremendous Trifles*. In life, there are a large number of tremendous trifles which we think are insignificant, even trivial. To be vigilant means to remember that they are tremendous.

It is so easy to get careless. Even responsible people sometimes forget to take care of little things, thinking that it is harmless. But if we can take care of the little things, we usually find that the big things will take care of themselves. It sounds trite, yet if we look carefully, we'll see that it is the person who takes care of little things day in and day out who makes progress.

In India, the man who trains the elephant is called the mahout. The mahout knows the elephant is a mighty creature that doesn't put up with any disrespectful treatment, but he knows the elephant's pressure points, so he uses these pressure points to train it. The mind too has many pressure points, and a sensitive one is the sense of taste – which makes it a good place to begin to train the mind by becoming vigilant where these tremendous trifles are concerned. It's not too difficult, and our taste buds can be good sports too.

Take those who are victims of compulsive eating – and who isn't at times? Suddenly you get a strong desire to eat something particularly unnourishing. At midnight you're awake for an hour, so you decide to go down to the kitchen and make a few cookies (chocolate chips, I understand, have a large clientele). You put on your slippers and tiptoe down the staircase without disturbing anybody. You're able to take down all the bowls and pans without making any noise at all. The dog doesn't even bark. It's all done so quietly and unobtrusively that you can legitimately say nobody has been adversely affected. It's all smooth, silent cooking. And afterwards everything is clean; there are no traces left so that others won't have any sense of jealousy in the morning. You might feel a little guilty for breaking your diet, but it's just a few cookies and that hardly counts. It hasn't inconvenienced anybody, it hasn't upset anybody, and after all, a few cookies are not going to make you overweight. But that isn't the problem we are talking about. Here the problem is quite different. By getting up from bed and yielding to that impulse at midnight, you have weakened yourself and undermined your security. When we have a craving at midnight for cookies, that is the time to be vigilant and not to yield.

There *is* a time to yield, on a special occasion, but we should not be the victim of a craving. I don't usually eat sweets, but now and then, when I go to the city with friends to celebrate a graduation or promotion, I like to go to a good place where we can have a treat. I am not going to take them somewhere that serves granola; I'm going to take them to a nice French bakery where they make the best chocolate cake this side of Paris. But there is no craving in this, and yet there is no loss of enjoyment. Whatever is done under the impulse of craving is painful. Whatever we do in freedom brings joy. That is why the Buddha says, "Don't act out of craving. Don't act out of attachment. Whatever you do, do it in freedom." That is the whole issue.

In this verse the Buddha uses the example of the elephant – people in India love elephants. Check your mind, the Buddha says. Be on your guard, and pull yourself out of a wrong situation as an elephant pulls itself out of the mud. When a dog gets into the mud, it just jumps right out because it is light. An elephant is heavy, and when an elephant gets into a swamp it finds it very difficult to get out. It struggles to pull itself halfway out and then falls back. You think it will never get free. But somehow the elephant has a way of almost throwing itself out, a bit like pulling yourself up by your own bootstraps. What the Buddha is recommending is like that: it's impossible, but you can do it.

> *An act performed carelessly, a vow not kept,*
> *a code of chastity not strictly observed: these*
> *things bring little reward. If anything is worth*
> *doing, do it with all your heart. A half-hearted*
> *ascetic covers himself with more and more dust.*
> [312–313]

TAKING AN ELEPHANT for a bath is an ambitious proj-ect. First, you must find a deep, wide pool. A little pond will not do. Then, once you get the elephant in, you have to spend a cou-ple of hours covering all the territory. The elephant likes a bath almost more than anything else, so when everything is finished and it's time to get out, the elephant will show you its ears so that you can wash behind them too. It's almost like he is saying, "Just here." Then he'll raise his leg, "What about the knee? There's a little spot there."

After all this scrubbing and cleaning, when the elephant finally gets out of the pool, all fresh and beautiful, the first thing he does is take up a trunkful of dust and throw it all over his body. The poor mahout has to take the elephant back into the pool all over again until the huge animal is clean enough to par-ticipate in the temple procession.

So the Buddha says don't look back. Keep your eyes on the goal. Otherwise you'll be like the elephant: you've had your bath and then thrown dust all over yourself, so you have to get back into the pool. There will be enough time only for getting into the pool, getting out of it, and getting in again.

What sound advice he gives! It seems obvious, but the enthu-siasm that pushes us to do something well from beginning to end, to work day after day at the task, is a precious quality that pays rich dividends. We must all have come across a person who starts a job with tremendous enthusiasm, only to have that enthusiasm fizzle out by the end of the week. The Buddha says such people will take a long time to cross the river of life, reminding us again and again that the ability to maintain continuing enthusiasm is a precious capacity we can all cultivate.

There are many ways in which we attack and undermine our enthusiasm. First is inconsistency. We may be enthusiastic by fits and starts. Our interest comes and goes, which causes endless confusion. For one week we are enthusiastic about archery. The next week it is flower arrangement. This month we want to try yoga, and next month we decide that Zen is our cup of tea.

On the spiritual path, most of us start with good intentions. We start out well, but then we waver. One day we are fired with enthusiasm for the spiritual life; on the following day our zeal has turned blue at the edges. Lack of sustained enthusiasm over many years causes nearly everyone problems. After an initial period of zeal, we find we make a slip. We do feel grieved for a short time, and then we make the slip again. Finally it becomes a habit. The only way to tackle this problem is to smile and overcome our resistance by an effort of will. When we start to vacillate, we can use that as an opportunity to become more steadfast.

If you do this regularly, you will become enthusiastic. When he was asked by one of his disciples, "Blessed One, how do I become selfless?" the Buddha said, "By trying to be selfless." Similarly, if we ask how to become enthusiastic, he might say, "By trying to be enthusiastic."

I have learned to expect a certain amount of beginner's

enthusiasm when people sit with me for meditation. For a month or two, or even longer, meditation goes smoothly. During this initial period, if I ask, "How is meditation going?" they usually reply, "It doesn't seem so very difficult. Maybe I have a natural aptitude for it."

I don't like throwing cold water on natural aptitudes, so it pains me to warn them that the easy early days will soon be over. Once you have learned to sink a little below the surface level of consciousness, you find an uncharted sea and realize you have no compass. At that time, if I ask, "Is your meditation still going well?" you will carefully reply, "Not exactly. I don't know where I'm going. I try to meditate, but all kinds of thoughts – from restaurants to jobs to movies to people – come and sit by my side throughout the meditation. I just don't know what to do."

Here we are, meditating earnestly, so how is it that a part of our mind is repeating a line from a song, while another part is remembering an important engagement we would rather forget? This double track of attention is likely to continue for a long time, but now we are beginning to understand that most of these thoughts come and go without our permission, and we begin to want to be masters in our own home. We renew our efforts in meditation, and thereby serve notice on the mind that we are going to be in the driver's seat at last.

As a blade of kusha grass can cut the finger
when it is wrongly held, asceticism practiced
without discrimination can send one on the
downward course. [311]

WHEN YOU TRY to pluck a blade of this particular kind of
grass, its razor-sharp edge will cut your finger badly if you are
not careful. We don't think of grass as cutting like a knife, so it is
only after we see the blood that we even know we have been cut.

When you hold any sharp instrument, if you are careless and
don't use it skillfully you can injure yourself and others. Similarly, the Buddha warns us that we have to be vigilant about certain things that can hurt a spiritual aspirant much more than
they would hurt someone else. After many years of meditation,
if you commit a serious lapse and suffer for it, you may be baf-
fled to see that a similar mistake committed by others may not
hurt them badly, whereas it has wounded you severely.

When you are walking on the lawn, if you fall down you may
not hurt yourself. You'll get a few bruises, maybe even twist your
ankle. But if you are repairing the roof and fall down, it will
cause you a serious injury. In meditation, through many years of
earnest endeavor, if we have climbed to a certain height, a serious fall can hurt us spiritually, emotionally, and even physically.
As we progress on the spiritual path the challenges become
more difficult, the temptations more problematic. It is important to make sure that we not put ourselves into a position where
a serious lapse can be committed, because the consequences can
be grave.

Some verses in the Dhammapada on this subject do sound
negative, even denunciatory. But coming from the compassion-

ate nature of the Buddha, such words are meant as a loving warning about how vigilant we have to be at all times in order to attain the supreme goal of nirvana. So these stern verses serve a useful purpose. Sometimes mistakes are committed not from bad intentions but from lack of care. For those who are earnest it is helpful to avoid situations where the passions are likely to be roused, until we have reached that state where the passions can be governed.

This does not mean that we need feel guilty or oppressed when we make mistakes. It's vital not to give in to an obsession with guilt, which can torment earnest people in the spiritual life, making existence miserable. We are not incorruptible; we can fall; we can have lapses. But there is no need for anyone to be depressed or despondent. If we build up self-doubt it can deplete our enthusiasm.

To quote our Bengali saint, Sri Ramakrishna, if you go on saying you are a sinner, you become a sinner. There are people who suffer so much from a guilt complex that it hampers their spiritual progress. This is one of the cleverest aces the mind can play. "You, you are no good. You, what can you say for yourself?" This dismal refrain can be a serious obstacle to meditation, which is why the mind does it. To get angry with oneself and reject oneself is not helpful and is not what the Buddha teaches. The best thing is not to say either "I'm all good" or "I'm worthless; I'm no good." The best thing is not to think about oneself, not talk about oneself, not dwell upon oneself at all – to be neither overconfident nor self-deprecating.

Self-examination has to be done with great detachment and compassion. It takes a great deal of detachment to see how imperfect we are and yet know that we can change our personality completely and rebuild it in the shining image of the Compassionate Buddha.

> Remember, this body is like a fragile clay
> pot. Make your mind a fortress and conquer
> Mara with the weapon of wisdom. Guard your
> conquest always. [40]

EVEN IF YOU have gone far in meditation – even if you are able to transform negative emotions into positive and ill will into good will – even then the Compassionate Buddha says to be vigilant, because there are powerful forces ready to oppose you. In Buddhism these negative forces are personified as Mara, the Tempter, the Striker. He is the personification of death and of every selfish passion, and he is always waiting because he never wants anyone to escape his kingdom. If you say, "I have become well established now; I don't have to meditate. I can afford to go into the marketplace and humor my passions because I am their master," Mara will be waiting to attack. The Compassionate Buddha says until you are completely established within yourself, there is a grave risk.

Mara is like one of those villains popular in films in India. After Jack the Giant has been knocked down and the referee is counting one, two, three, about to declare the winner, Jack slowly draws himself up and hammers the hero with a devastating blow. So this is one of the most valuable pieces of advice on the spiritual path: Don't ever become arrogant; don't ever become complacent. Never say, "Oh, Mara, who is he? Never heard of him." This is just what Mara likes to hear. He doesn't go near people who are always vigilant, people he knows are in fighting trim. He looks for the complacent fighter who has dropped his guard, let his muscles get flabby, and fallen asleep, quite certain that nobody is going to attack him. That is when Mara comes and hits him hard. Too late, the fellow leaps up and says, "You can't do this to me! Most people don't hit other people while they are asleep." Mara just says, "I'm not most people. I'm Mara."

Until we have entered nirvana, we must be careful about pitting ourselves against negative forces. We shouldn't lose our vigilance, and we shouldn't seek out a fight with Mara voluntarily. He will come without our asking. Today, we will lose the match with Mara, but one day we will become invincible. We have a sharp saying in Malayalam: "Whether the banana tree falls on the knife or the knife falls on the banana tree, it's the banana tree that suffers." Today you may be the victim, but eventually, when you are spiritually aware, whether you fall on Mara or Mara falls on you, it is Mara who will suffer. It's consoling advice for all of us, but it's also necessary for us to be vigilant in our spiritual disciplines and never miss meditation – never say, "Why not skip it this morning? Tomorrow I can make up."

> *Do not give your attention to what others do*
> *or fail to do; give it to what you do or fail to*
> *do.* [50]

VIGILANCE MEANS BEING aware of our shortcomings, but it does not mean we should dwell on them or get negative about ourselves or others. It was Saint Paul who gave a precise definition of confusion: Not doing things we should do and doing things we should not do. I don't think the world has ever improved upon this classic definition. Yet when it comes to vigilance, this is our usual state: we're very vigilant about others, but not about ourselves.

It is a curious thing, but most of us can be quite vigilant where others are concerned. We can practice sustained enthusiasm where the reformation of others is the goal. That is why the Buddha wisely adds a shrewd warning at this point. Instead of analyzing other people's defects – what they have done and what they have not done – isn't it more urgent to look at our own defects and start correcting them?

There is nothing very profound about this advice – until we try to practice it. Then we are likely to feel discouraged when we find that there are significant shortcomings in us. We begin to ask the belated question, "Me? How could I be so prone to error?" We may be embarrassed to find that the accurate response is, "To err is human." This is refreshing candor.

> It is easy to see the faults of others; we winnow
> them like chaff. It is hard to see our own; we
> hide them as a gambler hides a losing throw.
> But when one keeps dwelling on the faults
> of others, his own compulsions grow worse,
> making it harder to overcome them. [252–253]

BE ON GUARD, the Buddha says, but not against others. We are on guard forever and a day against other people, other communities, other races, other countries, and often we find what we are looking for. We are looking for wrongs and therefore we find them. Or we see a small fault and inflate it. On such occasions – if, for example, someone does me an injury that might prompt resentment to flow in my mind – I have found that if I can recall the good things that person has done, this quickly gives me a sense of proportion. Today David may present me with an angry word or even an unkind act, but if I look at my long association with David, I see that this is just one percent, a tiny fraction, of all the good words and actions he has given me over the years. For the time being, that one percent may weigh more than the ninety-nine percent – but only because of my wrong perspective.

Many relationships broken by this one percent could be rescued if we could recall that, yes, when I was ill she took care of me. When I was hungry he fed me. When I was discourteous he would bear with me. When I was prepared to attack her she forgave me. Soon, our sense of proportion has been restored.

> *Do not find fault with others, do not injure*
> *others, but live in accordance with the dharma.*
> *Be moderate in eating and sleeping, and*
> *meditate on the highest. This sums up the*
> *teaching of the Buddhas.* [185]

IT SEEMS TO be human nature to seek out the faults of others. Most of us go about looking for faults in other people. "Aha!" we say, "That Fred. I knew it." It may be some consolation when I see that Fred is full of faults because it enables me to excuse some of my own. Perhaps it gives me a momentary feeling of security.

On the other hand, we try to hide our own errors, even from ourselves. The Buddha asks us to look at the foolish gambler who tries to hide his throw. Ancient India had its version of Las

Vegas, and the Buddha's listeners would have understood immediately what he was talking about. Don't think that gambling is a modern invention. It was quite popular in India, and some of the royalty couldn't resist it, especially dice. In one famous scene in the *Mahabharata,* India's ancient epic, the hero loses his entire kingdom in a rigged game of dice. Here the Buddha says that it's futile to try to hide one's own problems by saying, "It's not me; it's him. It's not my fault; it's hers." This is like a gambler pretending he has an ace up his sleeve, but instead of an ace it's a joker.

In a personal altercation, especially in a tense situation, most of us will try to play this joker, the "not me" card. The Buddha asks, What does it matter who is at fault? What matters is the tragic estrangement that is taking place, and what is important is that the rupture should be healed.

In some situations, if someone is being unfairly critical of us, we may think the best defense is a good offense. But the Buddha's approach is vastly different. If someone is being critical of me, that is the time for me to be more appreciative. That is the way to calm the fault-finding person. It is just the opposite in much of the popular advice given today. If Romeo criticizes Juliet, she is urged to criticize him back. But how does this solve the problem? If it were a solution, I'm sure the Buddha would be all for hitting back. The responsibility is on the stronger, more secure person to be patient, to be considerate. This is the way to heal the relationship.

There are many, many ways of finding fault and deprecating others, some of them cleverly indirect. One of the most popular is damning with faint praise. It's an accomplished art in some circles, for example in politics. You pay a number of tributes to your worthy opponent and then you puncture all those balloons with a well-honed phrase.

Another approach, somewhat cowardly, is to convey gossip. Often gossipmongers protect themselves by claiming that they are speaking in the interests of truth. If Stuart has said something unpleasant about Bob, the gossiper must go and tell Bob every unfavorable thing that Stuart has said. There are people who will claim it's their duty.

I like my granny's way. She would leave the veranda when gossip started in our home, where our large joint family lived together and it wasn't possible to keep a secret for long. If it's not possible to leave the room, what I do is simple. Whenever I hear unkind words spoken about someone, I let them pass through – as you say, in one ear and out the other. If anyone sends malicious gossip into one ear, it goes straight through to the other ear without touching anywhere in between. This isn't an evasion of the truth. I am being loyal to the highest truth, which is to love one another.

It's not only the shortcomings of individuals that attract our critical eye. Other races and other nations can be included as well. It is interesting to listen to the conversation of a certain kind of tourist, who is generally disliked in all countries. His tacit assumption is that back home everything is so much better. The question anyone might want to ask is, "Then why don't you stay back home?"

It is not only tourists. Writers, economists, sociologists, and politicians may find it difficult to see that every country has its faults – including their own – just as every country has its own good points, including their own. Everywhere I have traveled, whether in India or Europe or the U.S., I have always tried to see the bright side. Every country has a bright side and every culture has a bright side. Yes, there is a dark side as well, but we can bear in mind that when the dark side is removed the bright side remains.

This is not a sentimental attitude that insists that every little town is ideal, every community is ideal, everybody is perfect. Sometimes I hear the expression, "Everybody is beautiful." The Buddha would say, "Everybody can *become* beautiful."

Out of a mistaken sense of charity, we may try to maintain the fiction that everybody is perfect. This is not what the Buddha means when he warns us not to seek the faults in others. We can be aware of difficulties in others, just as we are aware of difficulties in ourselves, but we should not sit in judgment on others because then we lose respect for them – and we lose respect for ourselves.

This is a distinction that requires some subtlety. Supposing you see a beautiful face and you concentrate only on the warts. I imagine even Cleopatra might have developed a wart or two. There are some people who will look for the imperfections. The beauty of Cleopatra's face is forgotten, all because of a small, almost invisible flaw.

There are others who refuse to observe at all. They do not understand the difficulties of other people – we needn't even call them defects; we can say difficulties – so they are disappointed before long. They have put on rose-tinted spectacles, but after a while the tint seems to wear out. Sadly, this is a serious cause of estrangement in romantic relationships, after the shining aura of the first period has faded. Most of us have gone through this intoxication in which our expectations and longings have distorted our eyesight.

It may sound prosaic, and no one wants to be a wet blanket where romance is concerned, but even in a romantic relationship, it's good to have a certain capacity for detached scrutiny. On the one hand, you observe all the assets; on the other hand, you are not blind to the liabilities. There are only a few who are capable of this early in life, but with experience we can all gradually develop this clear vision in which we are able to see the immense potential of every human being, while at the same time seeing the impediments to the realization of that potential. It's good to be aware of our own liabilities and be aware of others' liabilities, but we should never forget the hidden promise in us all – which includes the promise for attaining nirvana.

COMPETING WITH OTHERS makes us prone to self-criticism, which is a distortion of the healthy vigilance the Buddha teaches. Constantly comparing oneself with others is a debilitating state of mind. Often, those who have grown up in the atmosphere of competition are consumed by this inordinate need to compare themselves with others. It is a curious fact that when a competitive person acknowledges that he is at a disadvantage as compared to another person – whether in fact he is or is not – he then feels compelled to correct the balance by observing the other person's faults. For example, if John compares himself to Adam and feels he is intellectually or physically at a disadvantage, he may try to balance the scales by ferreting out some of Adam's faults. The mind, you must admit, is a clever customer, and this is just another way it has of confusing and agitating us.

This inveterate tendency of the mind to compare begins even in childhood. How many parents can't resist telling Junior, "Look at the boy next door. He scored three goals at the game today!" In my village every child heard this day after day. It was always, "Look at that boy – how good, how bright. Look at that girl – what a credit to her family." This was a favorite theme of every parent. When my grandmother heard these remarks she would tell me, "They must be saying the same about you. In the neighbor's home they must be saying, 'Look at the Eknath boy – so good, so bright, so promising.'" It comforted me very much.

There is no need for any one of us to compare ourselves to another person. All of us have our own potential. Instead of comparing ourselves with other people and getting miserable because we are not them, it is much more practical to realize our own gifts and talents.

> *If you hold yourself dear, guard yourself*
> *diligently. Keep vigil during one of the three*
> *watches of the night.* [157]

THE BUDDHA SAYS don't turn your shield against others, but turn the shield inwards. Don't keep watching others to see what they are up to. Mara is already inside, plotting your downfall, like those Greek soldiers that hid inside the wooden horse and emerged only when the Trojans were vulnerable to attack. That is what the Buddha is saying: We have let the danger come inside, so we must always be on guard, always vigilant.

*The disciples of Gautama are wide awake and
vigilant, with their thoughts focused on the
Buddha day and night.* [296]

THIS IS PERHAPS the most basic requirement of the
spiritual life: we need the inspiration of someone who has
crossed the river of life. Without the persuasive, encouraging
example of a rare man or woman who has achieved
enlightenment I don't think it is possible for any human being
to reach the other shore. The dangers are too great. The
endurance required is too enormous. And the other shore is
impossible to see. Yet inspired by the Buddha we can reach the
other shore if we follow the Noble Eightfold Path sincerely,
systematically, and with sustained enthusiasm.

*The disciples of Gautama are wide awake and
vigilant, rejoicing in meditation day and night.*
[301]

I DON'T MIND confiding in you that it takes many years to
be able to meditate joyfully. I understand the travail, but believe
me, there is no joy on the face of the earth equal to the joy I find
in meditation. I've known the pleasures of life, and I can firmly
say there is no joy like going deep, deep into your unconscious
and seeing a glimpse of the other shore. That is what this verse
really means. We meditate in order to descend into the depths –
not to dwell there, but to come back with great treasures. Those
who go deep, who are beginning to have some experiences in
meditation, are receiving a promise of much greater things to

come. Then those earnest souls who set out on the journey with confidence meditate with even greater enthusiasm, so that, in the words of the Buddha, they delight in meditation day and night.

Anyone who is sincerely leading the spiritual life can show that this is not a life in which color and joy are bleached out. Like the disciples of the Buddha of old, our daily life can show that we are cheerful and secure, able to face difficulties not only with equanimity but even with a certain restrained ebullience.

To make this journey, we needn't retire from the world. In fact, the world can hardly afford to lose anyone who is trying to lead the spiritual life. Their number is so small and the need is so great that such a person has a personal responsibility to make a small contribution in bringing peace to the world. When we know that our life is precious, when we know that the world needs our contribution, it will bring great motivation.

Let's end with a story.

The King of Kosala once said to the Buddha, "I have seen your students, and I have never seen such joyful people in all my life. They are like gazelles leaping in joy – so light, so graceful, so innocent. It does the heart good to look at them."

Perhaps the king was expecting monks to look sullen, even morose. That is why he tells the Buddha, "Your students have a light heart. They have a light foot. They have a gazelle's mind." Just look at a deer leaping across a meadow. The King of Kosala says, "When your students see obstacles, they just leap over them gracefully."

◇ *Finding the Courage*

ALONG THE MIGHTY crescent of mountains that runs from Pakistan to Nepal there are snow-clad peaks that beckon to mountaineers and pilgrims from every country on the face of the earth – men and women who want to test their endurance, to push their capacity to the utmost. On these high peaks, above twenty thousand feet, a physical curtain falls, and most ordinary human beings can live only for a few hours. Yet there are always a few – dauntless, determined, daring – who are prepared to make this most difficult, dangerous ascent.

I like to think of the Buddha, who was born in the far north of India in the shadow of these holy mountains, as a daring mountain guide, a spiritual sherpa who draws people who are not content to follow the petty, private urges of life. The vast multitude, those who live out their entire lives on the dusty plains, have been conditioned to content themselves with trifling satisfactions which they can hardly question. But in every country there are a few men and women who are prepared for the tremendous adventure that the Buddha places before us. They are tired of living in the valley of the shadow of death, and they find the pursuit of pleasure not wicked but boring. The pursuit of money is not just greedy, it's dull. These spiritual climbers have the same spirit as the British mountaineer George Mallory who, when he was asked why he climbed Mount Everest, gave the perfect answer: "Because it is there."

The Buddha really likes such tough, daring people, and his teaching is meant for heroes like these. This is neither morality nor philosophy; it is simply that if we follow the Buddha's way there will be challenges from beginning to end. At no time will we be able to sit back and say, "I am done."

So to the first quality required on the spiritual path, earnestness, the Buddha now adds a second: courage. By cultivating these two qualities all of us can go a long, long way – but first we must understand what the Buddha means by courage. Here courage means, first of all, endurance, which is just the opposite of what is often depicted as courage in movies and on television. For the Buddha, to be angry or revengeful is not courageous; it shows utter bankruptcy of courage. Today it's almost taken for granted that if you are not angry you are not strong; you are not tough. We have been brainwashed not to see bravery as it really is. It's a topsy-turvy world we live in, one in which we associate mere physical bravado with toughness and courage.

A few days ago I watched a film in which a gang fight was portrayed. These scenes are common in films: young men boasting of their courage and trying to provoke their rivals so they can overpower them with violence. But in this movie there was one young man who refused to fight in spite of every provocation. He was nonviolent, and he could not be frightened. I was so impressed I couldn't resist following my granny's example – she was known for expressing herself quite freely during performances – and saying out loud, "He is very brave!" I hope I didn't disturb the people in back. If you want to see bravery, look at the man or woman who can endure, who can be patient under attack, who will not retaliate, who will suffer rather than inflict suffering on another. That requires enormous courage.

When I was a little fellow, I was afraid of certain boys in my village who were notorious bullies. My fear of fighting them was not entirely because I was nonviolent; it was partly plain old cowardice. Seeing my difficulty, my granny came to my rescue by giving me a deep insight into violence. "Remember," she said, "violent people are cowards. Don't be afraid of them." It's good to understand that angry people are frightened people. We should take precautions and understand the danger, but at the same time, as my grandmother said, we should not live in fear. People without anger, who have great love, have inner courage.

> *Therefore, live among the wise, who are*
> *understanding, patient, responsible, and noble.*
> *Keep their company as the moon moving*
> *among the stars.* [208]

THESE ARE ALL qualities that can be cultivated and directed towards a higher goal. The word here for "wise" is *dhira,* which also means "one who is tough." It's an interesting combination of meanings. The Buddha isn't talking here about spiritual aspirants; he is talking about the person with guts. That's the real translation of *dhira.* If you have stamina, if you're really tough, if you can stick it out, then this is the teacher for you. He doesn't talk about the holy man, the saintly woman; he's talking about those who can "hang tough," to use a popular expression.

There is no lack of stamina in people today. There is no lack of daring in surfing, hang gliding, and rock climbing. But a thoughtful person would have to ask, To what purpose? What is the point of skydiving just to show how youthful we are? Daring and dedication are meant to be used for a higher purpose. The world today is not lacking in people with toughness and daring, yet often these qualities are used for personal profit, pleasure, and achievement. The same capacity to hang tough, to refuse to yield in the face of obstacles, can be harnessed in meditation – as it has to be if nirvana is to be achieved.

This is the toughness the Buddha shows when he sits under the bodhi tree and resolves, "Let my blood dry up! Let my body fall away! I will not get up from this place until illumination dawns." That is the spirit that is required, even by little people like us. It means no other goal will distract us, no obstacle will deflect us, because we want to reach the other shore so much we are not going to count the cost. When obstacles appear, people with this inward toughness find that all their fighting instincts come to their aid.

To think that nirvana is going to come to us by special delivery – that all we have to do is answer the door, take the package and open it, and there it is, nirvana – is to show an absurd misunderstanding of the Buddha's words.

When I go to San Francisco I like to visit Cliff House, with its beautiful view of the Pacific. Today I was watching the sea lions – portly, ponderous, pompous. There were about twenty of them in the waters swirling around the rocks below. For a long time they tried to climb up to bask in the sun, but each time one would go near the rocks, it would be pushed back by the crashing waves.

Those sea lions didn't say, "Let's give up and let the waves wash us out to sea." They came back again and again. Every time they were pushed away, they would disappear under the water and then come back to try again. I watched what persistence they have, what a fixed goal they clung to. At last one fellow made it. He lumbered up onto the top of a rock, lifted his head, and bellowed. I could almost hear him telling me, "You can put me in your book, and show people how they can succeed in meditation."

> Be like a well-trained horse, swift and
> spirited, and go beyond sorrow through faith,
> meditation, and energetic practice of the
> dharma. [144]

HERE THE BUDDHA uses the word *virya,* meaning full of energy, will, and courage. It's energetic practice that takes us forward, just as it's the spirited horse that wins the race. We need spirit, we need daring, for what could be more audacious than trying to cross the river of life?

And just a dash of wickedness, too, can help in a tight spot. "A dash of wickedness" means the daring that prompts us to experiment with something even if we know we may burn our fingers. In our younger days we all have a built-in margin for this kind of experimentation: to eat this, smoke that, sniff this, experience that. This type of person may have committed mistakes and caused some trouble; their name may be anathema at their old high school, and their hometown may pray they never come back. So be it. If they take to the practice of meditation and harness their need for adventure, such people can go like a swift steed to the goal.

> *Cross the river bravely; conquer all your*
> *passions. Go beyond the world of fragments*
> *and know the deathless ground of life.* [383]

WHEN I BEGAN teaching meditation in this country, in California in the nineteen-sixties, I found that the young people in my Berkeley classes, like most young people, looked for challenge, even risk. For them, to hear was to act. When an adventurous young man would hear that someone has jumped across the Grand Canyon on a motorcycle, he would immediately get on his motorbike and go riding about looking for the nearest canyon. If he falls, he gets another bike and tries another canyon.

In my village it was the same. We didn't have motorcycles, but there too teenagers were not afraid of a challenge. If somebody told us not to jump into the river from certain high rocks, we would immediately climb up and jump. So the Buddha says be like the teenager, who doesn't count the cost.

The Buddha is looking for people who have found that jumping over canyons and hang gliding are not daring enough, not challenging enough. Students of the Buddha want a challenge worthy of a human being, and they finally come to the conclusion there is no challenge on earth that can come up to crossing the river of life.

Turbulence, enthusiasm, enterprise, stamina – with these

qualities in abundance, young men and women respond deeply to the Buddha's message. This is why we are given a fighting spirit: not to fight against others but to fight against our own negative qualities, to "conquer all our passions, go beyond the world of fragments, and know the deathless ground of life."

Every ounce of resistance, rebellion, aggressiveness, and militancy we have will be used in this. Show me people who are really aggressive, really impetuous, and I will tell them that if they take to meditation they can go far. Even those who have negative qualities in generous measure can utilize those traits on the Buddha's path. If we have positive qualities, well and good. If we have negative qualities, also well and good. What more could we ask for?

> *As a strong wind blows down a weak tree,*
> *Mara the Tempter overwhelms weak people*
> *who, eating too much and working too little,*
> *are caught in the frantic pursuit of pleasure.*
>
> *As the strongest wind cannot shake a mountain,*
> *Mara cannot shake those who are self-*
> *disciplined and full of faith.* [7–8]

WHEN THE BUDDHA says someone is brave, he means that if that person is caught in a difficult situation he will not get diffident, she will not get dejected. For those with this kind of courage, the situation won't be utterly dark. They will find some way to use that situation for the benefit of others, even at the cost of some suffering for themselves. They will prefer to bear suffering themselves rather than inflict it on others.

There is only one way that is practical for all of us: to resolve that from today onwards, whatever it costs us, we will not let those around us suffer. The essential phrase is "whatever it costs." It is easy to agree up to a certain point: "Yes, up to a certain point I am prepared to suffer rather than bring suffering to others." But the Buddha would reply that "up to a certain point" is easy; what he is asking of us is all after the point. That's the whole fight. Up to a certain point there is no fight; it's just shadowboxing. The real fight begins after that point, when every animal instinct in us is crying out to strike back.

> Be victorious over yourself and not over others.
> When you attain victory over yourself, not even
> the gods can turn it into defeat. [104–105]

LIFE HAS A way of putting enemies in our path. Even the Buddha had enemies, but he chose to conquer himself rather than conquer others. In his own family, from his earliest days, there was another boy – a cousin named Devadatta – who was jealous of Siddhartha because of his goodness. Devadatta continued to be a thorn in Siddhartha's side all his life. Devadatta fought others and lost. The Buddha fought himself and won nirvana.

When they were boys, Devadatta couldn't sleep because of the perfection of his cousin. As they entered manhood, another reason was added for Devadatta's hatred: he too wanted to marry Yashodhara, who chose Siddhartha instead. For him his rival was not the "Compassionate Buddha" but the man who got his girl. Though Devadatta eventually entered the order and was even said to have attained supernormal powers through his austerities, he grew to be a bitter man, constantly plotting against the Buddha. Devadatta never learned that when we fight against others we always lose.

One day, driven by hatred, he released a cobra into the hermitage where the Buddha was meditating. Death from cobra bite is almost immediate, and Devadatta returned the next day expecting to see the Blessed One lying dead. Instead, he saw the cobra, the messenger of death, with its hood raised over the Buddha to protect him from the burning rays of the sun.

Don't think that Devadatta was a mediocre aspirant. He had outstanding qualities that attracted the admiration of other dedicated monks and even princes. Even Ajatashatru, the son of King Bimbisara, the ruler of Magadha, was impressed by the magic powers of the monk Devadatta and became his devoted disciple. It was to be a tragic association between the prince and the monk, for they began to plan together how they could seize power for themselves.

They hit upon a sinister plan: Devadatta would become the head of the order and Ajatashatru would replace his father on the throne of Magadha. When he heard rumors of this tragic plot, rather than oppose his son, King Bimbisara abdicated, for he was deeply drawn to the Buddha and wanted to follow the spiritual life. He installed Ajatashatru as ruler, saying, "This is what you want, so I give it to you."

Bimbisara left the palace with his mind at peace, but Devadatta still thought of him as a threat. So day after day Devadatta urged Ajatashatru to imprison his father. Soon it came to pass as Devadatta desired, and Bimbisara was imprisoned by his son. On that day, because of his evil thoughts,

Devadatta lost all of his supernormal powers. Also on that day Devadatta began in earnest to fulfill his plan to become master of the order.

Knowing that he had the support of King Ajatashatru, and thinking that the Buddha was now old and incapable of resistance, Devadatta went to the assembly of the monks and said that it was time for the old man to find peace by retiring to the forest, leaving Devadatta in charge. The Buddha replied quietly that he wouldn't consider putting even Sariputta or Moggallana in charge, much less Devadatta. But, as we have seen, Devadatta was not lacking in magnetism, so when he invited the monks to leave the Buddha and follow him, many listened.

After a few days, the Buddha sent Sariputta and Moggallana to bring back these foolish monks, who by that time were eager to rejoin the Buddha. When Devadatta discovered all the monks had left him, he fell ill. Knowing he was about to die, he wished to see the Buddha one last time and started on the journey in a litter because he was too weak to walk. On his journey, according to the chronicles, he asked that the litter be placed on the banks of a pond, and when he stepped out to wash, the earth opened and quicksand swallowed him. It was his fate, the sutras say, to be reborn in a hellish world because of his great misdeeds. But as he was dying he called on the Buddha for refuge, and therefore the immense burden of his karma was lightened to a great extent.

Ajatashatru too repented of his evil deeds after the death of his father. The same fear was now haunting his mind that he had caused in his father's mind. As he grew older he had no peace and was tormented by terrifying dreams. Finally, in great fear, he went to the Buddha, who received him kindly and listened to his confession. The Buddha eased the king's mind, bestowing peace upon him, but after he departed, in great sorrow the Compassionate One told the monks that if Ajatashatru had not been guilty of such great crimes he would have gone far, far along the path to enlightenment in that very life. The Buddha said, "He is a man wounded by his own arrow."

The sad story of Devadatta teaches an age-old lesson: as long as we attack others under the foolish belief that the enemy is outside, we can never be victorious. The real enemy is within all of us. This is the enemy we have to face with courage and then defeat. Gird yourself up to fight, the Buddha would say; the battle is already joined! Don't try to run away. The enemy is all that is base in us, all that is greedy, selfish, and separate. This is the real enemy, who hides within and deceives us by warning, "Look out! The enemy is waiting for you outside."

> *One who conquers himself is greater than*
> *another who conquers a thousand times a*
> *thousand men on the battlefield.* [103]

THOSE WHO HAVE conquered ten thousand enemies, what glory do they have? What valor? Those who conquer themselves, who conquer every vestige of selfishness and separateness in their hearts, are the real conquerors, because their life is victorious.

Many spiritual teachers use the language of war as the Buddha does now. Mara, who represents all the forces of darkness, is ranged against you. Don't try to avoid the fight, because it is inescapable. You cannot afford to withdraw from the fight. You cannot say, "I'm going to drop out, get into a cave, and put up a sign saying Nobody Here." You cannot avoid fighting, but you can choose the enemy. If you choose to fight others, heads you lose, tails you lose. If you choose to fight yourself, heads you win, tails you win.

One who has conquered a thousand times a thousand people is no conqueror. He has brought only misery to a thousand times a thousand people, laid waste the land, broken the hearts of widows and children. How can such a person claim to be victorious? It's a cruel question, which should force us to rewrite history and remove titles like "conqueror" and "great" from those who attacked other nations or exploited other races. Only if you have wiped out every trace of selfishness from your consciousness, the Buddha says marvelously, can you call yourself a hero.

I DON'T WANT to cast a veil on the truth that as we travel towards nirvana and get into the deeper levels of consciousness, challenges become more difficult, temptations become more damaging. In my observation, it takes many years for a good meditator to reach the point in the inner journey where these struggles take place. In India the traditional period is twelve years, but that was for ancient times; conditions are more difficult today. Indeed, there are benefits to taking a long time, because nothing on earth is more demanding than this journey, even for those with abundant courage.

In any case, whether it takes twelve years or twenty, the time will come when we find ourselves halfway across the sea of samsara, which means we've reached a point of no return. At this juncture, to speak frankly, there is no going back. If we try to turn back we will drown. The time when we could indulge in private pursuits and personal peccadilloes is long past; now our safety depends on the courage to go forward. At this threshold, if we harbor any reservations in our consciousness, it can be a source of great danger. Compromise is no longer possible. We must fight and win.

Simply reaching this point means we have won many battles, but powerful negative forces remain in our way. It is these negative samskaras that we now face. We have trained for years, we can consider ourselves proven warriors, but the samskaras we now face are strong and extremely well trained, ready to fight at any time. But there can be no complaining, no running away. If you feel inadequate and try to run, you are defeating the very purpose for which all your meditation has been undertaken. There is only one way to learn to fight samskaras, and that is by fighting.

For many, the key samskara to face at this time is an overpowering temptation. Almost no one is a stranger to this. When a great wave of passion rises up in our deeper consciousness, a passion that we find difficult to control, we can look to the example of the saints and sages of all religious traditions and see that it can be conquered and harnessed. The point is to have free choice. There are some rare people who get a great deal of joy in fighting a samskara. I confess I am one of them. There is a certain amount of sheer bravado in this which appeals to me deeply. The Buddha had this kind of courage, of course, but so did gentle, lovely Yashodhara – and Kisa Gotami, Ananda, and the other disciples of the Buddha.

Those who are vigilant, who train their minds
day and night and strive continually for
nirvana, enter the state of peace beyond all
selfish passions. [226]

NOW THE BUDDHA is really getting down to the basics of the spiritual struggle by using the word *asava,* which can be freely translated as "selfish passion." These are our mortal foes, not anyone or anything outside, and we will come face to face with them, and eventually vanquish them, in the practice of meditation. Even half an hour every morning and half an hour again every evening helps little by little to establish victory.

In our own meditation, if we go deep enough, when the time is right we are going to come face to face with the long-nourished ferocity of our own cravings. It can throw us into great anxiety, confusion, and even panic. I don't think anyone can escape this encounter, which will test every ounce of resolution and courage we have. Only when we realize the difficulty of bringing our passions under control – discovering how impossible it seems to transform anger into sympathy, ill will into good will, hatred into love – do we see why the Buddha's teaching is meant for heroes.

For a long, long time in this struggle we are going to get unpleasant hits from our opponent, personified as Mara. We have to study this opponent as best we can, and for a long time it's mostly guesswork. We have to learn when the mind is likely to go out of control. What are the circumstances in which a particular asava overcomes you? When this urge comes over you, how do you act? How do you speak? Who gets the brunt of it? And how long does it last?

The first time we confront a strong selfish passion, it can be frightening. Let me assure you, everyone will have the same reaction: a desire to forget the whole thing. Everyone asks, "How can I fight against this? It is a part of myself! Where am I going to get the resources and the strength for this struggle?" This is where the Compassionate Buddha says, "Draw yourself up and declare, 'Come friend, come foe, send storms and hurricanes, I will not be afraid.'"

All of us have a natural sympathy for the little fellow who fights back against someone big. There is some curious satisfaction in supporting an underdog pitted against a giant. So it is with the Buddha-to-be defying Mara. As Siddhartha takes his vow under the bodhi tree on the night preceding his awakening, it does look for a time like the story of David and Goliath. Mara, the embodiment of ignorance and suffering, loomed over him like Goliath. It was a long, bloody fight, but such was the Buddha's will and courage – so strong, so invincible – that at last the victory was his.

Those who begin to understand the daring involved in facing cravings will find that their imagination can catch fire. If your cravings can be described as a bull, there you are, a matador in the ring. At any moment you don't know if you will be gored. It's so terribly difficult to say no. The very definition of a craving is that you will not be able to say no; if you could say no, it would not be a craving. It takes real daring to be able to say no when the bull is charging. But if you can say that consistently and mean it, you have won.

If one who enjoys a lesser happiness beholds
a greater one, let him leave aside the lesser to
gain the greater. [290]

PEOPLE WHO YIELD to their cravings immediately, who cannot wait patiently for a greater satisfaction, are lacking in courage. Even to resist a small craving – for food, for example – is an act of courage. Giving up your favorite cup of coffee is an act of heroism.

When we have defeated one obstacle like this, the next one has got to be bigger – and the one after that has got to be bigger still. As our muscles get stronger, the obstacles become greater and the challenges more difficult. After all, until we are able to surmount a smaller obstacle, there is no point in trying to clear another that is more formidable. Little by little we get a period of training that enables us to tackle bigger and bigger challenges.

In the deeper stages of meditation, we enter a subterranean world where we can see some of our strongest samskaras – positive and negative – including some of our greatest failings. When we come face to face with these, looming over us like a leviathan from the depths, we must be able to deal with them successfully, not only with detachment but with skill.

Take the question of jealousy, for example, which in a competitive society has become rampant. Jealousy is a universal samskara today. I see a lot of jealous people here, just as I did in India – among students, among faculty, among secretaries, among janitors. We have jealousy far and wide, but I didn't understand the nature of jealousy until my meditation deepened and I gained some insight into the samskaras of the personal unconscious. Then, whenever I saw jealousy on my campus, I began to understand that it wasn't jealousy of one particular person. It is simply jealousy – full stop.

When Alfred is jealous of Bill, for example, he is thinking, "If only I can compete successfully with Bill, I will be free from this jealousy that torments me." What happens is quite different. Yes, Alfred may compete successfully with Bill, but he will become more jealous rather than less, because there is Christopher just waiting to appear on the scene. It is absurd to connect jealousy with just one person. If Albert has a jealousy samskara, it will always be lying dormant, waiting for someone to set it in motion. In other words, even to say that Albert is jealous of Bill is not correct. "Albert is jealous" is the correct statement.

There is only one way to tackle this samskara: to use that very jealousy itself as an opportunity to set it right. It's a remarkable application of the Buddha's teaching to go against the current. When you are jealous of a particular person, that is the time to be kind to that person, move closer, and learn to work together in harmony. This is why the Buddha uses the word *dhira*, "tough." When you try to avoid someone because of jealousy, you are being timid. When you feel upset because of jealousy and don't try to overcome it, you're being cowardly. In using the word *dhira*, the Buddha says we must find the courage, the daring, to be kind to those of whom we are jealous. This is how to face the samskara and conquer it.

THE SPIRITUAL LIFE is a battle, and when you say you are not going to speak to someone, you have fled the battlefield. If you say you are not going to sit near someone, not going to work with someone, you're back in your tent.

Once you reach this stage in meditation, if a problem like this comes up you can't run away. You can't say you'd rather stay home. You have to take it on. This is what you have been training for. When someone is unkind to you, you must try to be kind in return, whatever the cost. When someone doesn't like working with you, you need to do your best to work in harmony with that person. These are the acts of heroes and heroines, which were favorite words of my granny.

In an affectionate mood – partly teasing me, partly challenging me – my granny would sometimes ask, "Don't you want to be a hero?"

I would reply, "Thank you, Granny, no." It took years to discover, as my meditation deepened, that I could face the threats of the ego rather than run away. How many times I have said I'd rather die than give up! And I meant it. The ego tried to frighten me in all kinds of ways: "Your health will go to pieces. You won't be able to function. You won't be able to teach." In the language of the Buddha, this was the voice of Mara. Finally I learned to answer, "What do I lose?" I make no claim to be a naturally brave man, but the thought of running away was something I could not tolerate.

Some of our samskaras are so fierce that the battle can go on for months, even years. You get beaten up, but you come back to fight again. The samskara says, "Look at your condition. It's pathetic." You say, "I agree, but I am going to come back at you again until you're sent against the ropes." And you come back again and again until the samskara is beaten. That's the fight with a samskara. So whenever someone comes to me and complains of having a lot of trouble, I have to give them Job's consolation: that's what fighting against a samskara means.

Ultimately, it's not fighting one samskara and then another and then another that brings us to the other shore that is nirvana. There is no one tougher than the Buddha, who asserts that ultimately, in order to reach nirvana, we must leave behind our identification with all of the skandhas – not only the body, but the mind and intellect too.

When I began the practice of meditation I was holding a responsible professorship at a large university in India. At that time I wanted to share my love of beauty with all the students who were eager to learn, so I was quite sure this was the road I would travel for the rest of my life. Then the ground shifted under my feet. I remembered what my grandmother had told me years before, that my life wasn't going to be like anybody else's. I had forgotten all about that statement and I had never understood what she had meant, but now her words seemed prophetic. At the very apex of my career, everything I had worked for – money, position, prestige – lost its flavor.

In today's world it requires a good deal of daring to begin to reject the claims that are made on behalf of the intellect. In my case, because I had been brought up in a world in which the intellect was always honored, in my early days I could not even have begun to understand the Buddha's call to go beyond intellectual knowledge. So I could easily sympathize with the attitude of my colleagues in the English department who looked upon medita-

tion as a kind of intellectual suicide. Today I can easily understand the horror people feel when they are told that the intellect
is not the highest instrument of knowledge, and the panic they
feel when the Buddha says we must still the mind and lay the
intellect aside in order to awake to a higher mode of knowing.

> *Selfish attachment brings suffering; selfish*
> *attachment brings fear. Be detached, and you*
> *will be free from suffering and fear.* [212]

IT IS NATURAL to play for a while in reasonable measure
with the toys of life – the games of personal pleasure and personal profit. But once we begin to grow dissatisfied with these
toys, we shouldn't wait for them to be snatched away; we should
throw them away willingly. It's going to be painful, and at first
there will be a sense of deprivation, but all of them can be
thrown away, and when they are, we get the taste of freedom.

Of course, this can go in fits and starts. A lot of people put
their toys aside but then go searching in the grass to see whether
they can be recovered. I can sympathize, because there is a difficult interval after we have thrown these things away in order to
cross the river but haven't yet come in sight of the other shore. It
can really be an awful time.

The capacity to throw away something to which we are
attached is called in Sanskrit *vairagya* – detachment, renunciation. There is a close link between detachment and courage, a
kind of catch-22: if you have the courage you can throw the toy
away, and if you can throw the toy away you gain in courage.
Another way of saying it is: you will never have courage until

you have detachment, and you will never have detachment until you have courage.

A verse from the Indian poet Bhartrihari, who had a strong vein of renunciation, reveals this connection between courage and detachment. Bhartrihari says even the bravest of us live in a world of fear:

> In pleasure there is fear of disease;
> In a good family, fear of disgrace;
> In wealth, fear of taxes;
> In honor, fear of humiliation;
> In power, fear of enemies;
> In beauty, fear of old age;
> In learning, fear of contradiction;
> In virtue, fear of scandal;
> In the body, fear of death.
> All things of this world are mixed with worry.
> Renunciation alone brings freedom from fear.

Trying to find security in anything that changes subjects us to terrible fears. And ultimately, Bhartrihari says, we fear death itself – because of our identification with the body. Even for the bravest, therefore, life is full of fear. Even if we don't accept it or say we are not aware of it, everything generates fear. So Bhartrihari ends by echoing the Buddha: only detachment – *vairagya* – can bring freedom from fear.

When we come to understand this and seek the path of renunciation, we may want to say, "Well, Blessed One, first put your hand in mine; then I'll drop these toys." The Buddha replies, "You drop the toys; then I'll put my hand in yours."

We say, "Yeah, yeah, I'm throwing." And the Buddha waits to see.

But there is a rare kind of man or woman who is able to renounce with abandon even when the mind says, "Don't throw it away! Keep it!" I can't tell you how this is done, but there are a few people who are able to do it. While the mind is saying, "Alas, I lost it, I lost it!" the heart says, "You lost it? Silly fellow, you have won everything."

WE ARE PLAYING a dangerous game in trying to cross the river of life. It takes not only courage but preparation. It's foolish to try to undertake such a challenge without undergoing disciplines – physical, mental, and spiritual.

During the monsoon the boys in my village liked the challenge of swimming across the flooded river. But we knew the dangers. First and foremost, we had to decide that we were going to cross the river; then we would wade in slowly, step by step, to see how strong the current was. Finally, before getting into the depths, we'd pick a landmark to aim for on the other side. It's a delicate calculation to judge the strength of the current and how much to allow in order to arrive exactly at the opposite point on the other side.

You don't plunge into a river that is too deep and too swift for your strength. Similarly, don't place yourself in situations where your samskaras will be nourished and strengthened. Don't let yourself get entangled in a situation in which you are likely to lose your power of observation. In such a situation you cannot fight because you are riding on the samskara's back. "Where is that samskara?" you ask. The samskara says, "Who do you think is under you?" You want to get off and fight the samskara, but you can't.

AS I SAID earlier, I wasn't a particularly brave boy. I had quite a number of fears – for example, the fear of ghosts, which is widespread in India. Every village has its special ghost, and sometimes there is even a competition for the most dramatic local ghoul. I was also afraid of cobras – a fear instilled early in Kerala because it's a necessary safeguard. Most other boys shared this fear, but I remember one fellow who, instead of running away when he saw a snake, would pick it up by its tail and then swing it around. That's what you can do to a samskara if you have enough daring and enough skill and have gone far enough in meditation: you can pick up a samskara by its tail and just throw it away.

But this is a feat that we can accomplish only when our meditation is really deep. In the case of ordinary people like you and me, it is more helpful to think of ways we can starve the samskara. We start by not putting ourselves in situations where the samskara will get fed, lodged, and exercised. When the samskara becomes weak and cannot crawl, we can take it on. This may not sound very brave, but it's effective.

In my high school I had two boon companions from my ancestral family. One was a cousin who was well known for liking trouble. He would go out of his way to meet with the troublesome people in our village, even choosing to go down the street where they lived, but he was never attacked. My other companion was noted for being quiet. He never interfered with anyone. He never provoked anybody, but he didn't like to be provoked either, and everyone knew that when he was provoked he would do dangerous things. He too was never challenged, even when he went down those same streets.

As for myself, I never went that way at all. If necessary I just went around. So none of us were ever attacked. But I saved a lot of energy, which even the friend who liked trouble admitted to me later on.

In the latter stages of meditation, when we come face to face with our samskaras, those who don't like trouble can avoid temptation. We can learn to recognize when we don't have enough fighting capacity to tackle it head on. Why take on a tyrant samskara you can't manage? Wait until the bully is sick and weak, then jump on him. This may not be playing by Queensbury rules, but samskaras don't play by rules at all. Weaken your samskaras, the Buddha would say; then, if necessary, hit below the belt.

> *The disciples of Gautama are wide awake and vigilant, absorbed in the dharma day and night.*
>
> *The disciples of Gautama are wide awake and vigilant, with their thoughts focused on the sangha day and night.* [297–298]

IT IS NOT possible for the average human being to wage a constant struggle below the conscious level, but in the practice of meditation, little by little, we can begin to take on our samskaras. We may be no match for Mara at first; that I concede. But at least we can go and trample on some samskara's tail. We may not do much harm to the samskara at first, but we have landed a blow. The feeling of triumph will stay with us. It will prove to us that there are unsuspected reserves that we can draw on in this fight. Day by day we are giving notice to the samskara that the struggle will go on until we achieve victory.

All the resources we need are right within each of us. I want to assure you of this over and over again: every one of us has these resources within ourselves. No one should say, "I am what I am, and there is nothing I can do about it." There is everything we can do.

Once we are beyond the beginning stages in meditation and enter deeper levels of the mind, we will feel at times that we don't have the dedication and the courage to go further. When these feelings of inadequacy come, we can find a source of encouragement in the faith and endurance of our spiritual teacher. A trusted spiritual guide can always tap us on the shoulder and say, "You had better avoid that" or "Please don't do that again." When the time comes to confront a deep, lifelong samskara, it can affect the body, disturb the mind, cloud the judgment, sap the will. That's when the Buddha can come into the ring with you as your second, sitting in your corner with a towel and a pat on the back to urge you back for another round.

Another source of strength is what in Buddhism is called the *sangha*. The term used in Sanskrit is *satsang*, which derives from two smaller words: *sat*, meaning the good or truth or reality, and *sanga*, group or association. Thus it signifies the seekers of the highest, banded together. It is very, very difficult to go it alone on the spiritual path, and most teachers, like the Buddha, say we should travel together with a few friends following the same path. That's the value of satsang. Don't plow a lonely furrow.

When you are able to work with others harmoniously and treat them with unfailing kindness, you slowly gain confidence. When you learn to work cheerfully and harmoniously even with those you find difficult, you are gaining courage for the journey.

Compared to the vast, uncharted sea of consciousness that we cross in meditation, external exploits pale into insignificance. This adventure is true joy. Pleasure, however keen, is very short, very limited; therefore it is at best only a kind of fake joy. The Buddha says joy arises from meeting a great spiritual challenge. Joy comes with your mastery of the skills that enable you to meet the challenge. In other words, the Buddha is presenting us with a daring, difficult, and dangerous way of living.

It is the effort itself that brings joy, not the results. Every day is fresh for you; every moment is fresh for you. When you learn to fight the battle the Buddha is talking about, the joy is permanent. The mastery is permanent. Those who learn to fight their passions win a joyous victory. These fighters have an abiding sense of triumph, and they have an abiding sense of happiness.

ONLY A HANDFUL have the inner daring, the spiritual audacity, and the resoluteness of will required for reaching the other shore. When Buddha the Boatman comes to this shore where we are all running up and down, he says graciously, "I am on my way to the other shore, friend! There are a number of vacancies in the boat. In fact, almost every seat is available. Why don't you just get in and sit down. I'll take you across."

A few daring travelers do get into the Buddha's boat, but most of us find that our attachments to money and possessions, to pleasure and power and prestige, prevent us from accepting the Buddha's invitation, which is always open. Everybody has received this invitation, and when our eye of wisdom begins to open we can read it. "No RSVP. Casual clothes. Be at the dock early morning." Nobody can complain, "I haven't been invited." But selfish attachments will be inspected carefully. As Shakespeare would say, there's the rub.

> *Bhikshu, empty your boat! It will go faster.*
> *Cast out greed and hatred and reach nirvana.*
> [369]

THE BUDDHA'S BOAT is for sailing, to take you from this shore to the next. So why do you keep adding ties? Why do you keep adding all kinds of attachments? Why do you add to your luggage, your cravings? You have made the sailboat into a houseboat that will never put out to sea. Don't you want to get into the sea, where the whales play, where the waves rise high? Don't you want to thrill to the voyage? That is what life is for.

In order to sail across the sea of samsara to the other shore of love eternal, beyond all change, we have to transform everything that is negative in us into what is positive, everything that is selfish into what is selfless. This takes many, many years of arduous endeavor, as we learn to turn every selfish relationship into a selfless one and break the fetters that tie us to this shore.

This is the topic of the next chapter, in which we will find out what the Buddha means by breaking attachments and learning to love selflessly.

◇ *Love for All*

I HAVE SEEN fascinating scholarly conjectures as to where the Biblical Garden of Eden might lie on the map, but to me Eden is much more than a place. It represents a state of consciousness: that state in which we transcend our physical separateness to live in the indivisible unity that the Buddha calls nirvana.

Entering this state is the goal of all religions, which are founded upon the experience of unity as realized by a noble spiritual figure such as Jesus or the Buddha. As Swami Vivekananda said, "Religion is realization." It has very little to do with philosophy or metaphysics or theology; it is the realization with every cell of our being that all life is one.

This continuous awareness of unity, and not separate physical existence, is our native state. Mystics speak of it as the soul's true home. In the evolution of consciousness, it is not only the state of being from which we come, but also that to which we must one day return, not in some afterlife but here on earth, by discovering in our own consciousness our oneness with the rest of life. It's a useful reminder for all of us, when we are faced by our negative attitudes or selfish desires, that our nature – what

Buddhists call our Buddha-nature – is to be good, to be kind, to be selfless. In other words, we are all impostors, pretending to be selfish, pretending to be violent. By nature we are all, each of us, the expression of the ultimate truth and love.

In this sense, our fall from unity into this delusion that we are separate, limited, purely physical creatures is not an event that took place one day in the distant past. It is still going on. Just as cosmologists say they can pick up faint echoes of the primeval big bang with which the universe began, a sensitive observer can pick up echoes of the fall into disunity and disharmony, which continues every day in all our lives.

All valid spiritual disciplines – in Judaism and Christianity, Islam and Zoroastrianism, Hinduism and Buddhism – are meant to end in the realization of unity. To put it positively, the purpose of spiritual discipline is to learn to love all. For most of us this means living with our family and gradually extending that love to every other person and creature on the face of the earth.

From another point of view, the purpose of spiritual discipline is to extinguish self-will once and for all, because all that stands between us and the awareness of unity is this self-centered conditioning that we are separate creatures. This is the most literal meaning of the word *nirvana*: *nir* out, *vana* to blow. It is the extinction not of self but of self-will, which the Dhammapada personifies as Mara.

They leave darkness behind and follow the light.
They give up home and leave pleasure behind.
Calling nothing their own, they purify their
hearts and rejoice. Well trained in the seven
fields of enlightenment, their senses disciplined
and free from attachments, they live in
freedom, full of light. [87–89]

FOR THOSE THE Buddha is talking about here – those who leave darkness behind and follow the light – the world of multiplicity dissolves; the world of separateness falls away. They no longer see people as separate, no longer see any form of life as separate. They see everyone, every creature, as one appearing to be many. This is what nirvana means: the extinction of the limited frontiers of the ego.

When we attain nirvana, we discover simultaneously that we and the universe are one. Afterwards, we order our life in such a way to express this oneness. We come to have love for everybody, so our love is multiplied billions of times. When we hear of the people of other countries suffering, we feel as grieved as when those in our own country suffer. There is no difference at all. War is ruled out, violence is ruled out, exploitation is ruled out; everybody becomes our kith and kin. In the Buddha's words, we live "for the welfare of the many, live for the happiness of the many" – *bahujana hitaya, bahujana sukhaya.*

In order to live for the welfare of all, of course, our personal life has to be transformed. But this can be done naturally, beautifully, right in the midst of family and friends. In order to follow the light we don't have to go to another country or leave our job or family. Living with others is a very valuable aid to the spiritual life, because that is where we start learning slowly to forget ourselves more and more in the welfare of those around us. Difficult parents or difficult children, a difficult partner or a difficult friend or co-worker – all these relationships are opportunities for learning to love. When the wonderful day dawns when we are more concerned with the welfare of others than with our own, we "live in freedom, full of light."

It is a long, long journey to nirvana. Unselfishness and even self-sacrifice are often called for, but day by day we can extend our love to include all. This can be done – must be done – with those nearest to us. We don't take a globe and say, "Let me embrace you." This is the intellectual approach, but it doesn't always translate into daily practice. We should be wary of people who say they embrace the cosmos and feel at one with every creature. I appreciate much more those whose eyes light up when they see their parents or partner. Unless you have learned to be selfless in your own family, you do not have the opportunity to develop the skill by which you can include all creation in your love.

We do not have to drop out of society. In meditation we retire inside in order to leap forward. Just as a long jumper goes a long way back in order to get the momentum to run and leap forward, when we meditate we go deep into our consciousness to get the power to leap into life to tackle problems and solve them successfully. The purpose of the Buddha's life was to make the whole world a better place. Perhaps our small purpose, on a scale suitable for ordinary people like us, is to make our family a better place, our city a better place – yet, by walking in his footsteps, I believe that we too can make a contribution to our world, to make it a better place for our children to grow up in.

Let us live in joy, never attached among
those who are selfishly attached. Let us live in
freedom even among those who are bound by
selfish attachments. [199]

AFTER HE ATTAINED illumination, the Compassionate Buddha returned home in his saffron robes and walked down the streets of Kapilavastu with the dignity of the royal prince that he was. Yet his father, blinded by attachment, could see only the poor rags of a monk, the miserable face of a mendicant. So enraged that he forgot his royal dignity, the king accosted his son saying, "You have brought dishonor to our family. You have disgraced our history."

Gently, the Buddha bowed to his father and addressed him with respect. "How have I brought you shame?"

"You are now a beggar wandering along the streets of our royal city, where my father and grandfather and great-grandfather ruled."

"It is the way of all Buddhas, those born in the past and those to be born in the future, to seek alms from everyone," the monk replied. "You describe your dynasty, but I know that my lineage extends far beyond earthly kings. All creatures are now my family. I come from that from which all of us come, in which all of us exist, and to which all of us will return."

Hearing the melodious voice of the Buddha and seeing his loving gaze, the king felt his anger depart.

"Father," the Buddha said, "let me give you the wisdom of the dharma."

The king and the Buddha walked along together and the Buddha taught his father about the path he had found, and the king's eyes were opened. For the first time he understood that it was the destiny of his son to become a Buddha, and it brought him a deep joy.

THE BUDDHA DRAWS a careful distinction between selfless love and selfish attachment, because the first will be an aid to our spiritual progress and the second will be an obstacle. Yet it is necessary to be careful with the word *attachment*. In practice it may be more helpful to think of right attachment and wrong attachment. In the first, you put the happiness of others first; in the second, you put your own happiness first, which means it is an expression of self-will. Even in personal attachments, if you keep putting the other person first, eventually you will be free – if you can love that person deeply and be loved by that person deeply. In wrong attachment, you are going to be bound, and you are going to make the other person bound as well, and eventually even hostile.

The Buddha is not disapproving of our love for those around us, and he is certainly not discouraging us from loving. His teaching is about cultivating a love that is not subject to change, a love that will always be with us. In the first flush of emotion, when we say, "I love you," this does express what we feel for that person at the time. But true love takes time to develop. As we grow spiritually, we can look forward to the great day when the other person's welfare and happiness mean more to us than our own. Then we can say with conviction, "I do love you."

Compulsive attachment is often mistaken for something that is good and lasting, but it is neither. A compulsive attachment promises to bring satisfaction but delivers dissatisfaction, promises to bring joy but delivers sorrow. That is why, although the word *detachment* in English has a negative sound, detachment brings better health of body and mind, longer life, and greater creativity.

In following the way of the Buddha we are not turning our back upon our own happiness or the happiness of our nearest and dearest. We are including everybody in our search for joy and fulfillment. We are not turning our back upon our own happiness; it is included in the happiness of the whole, of which we are a part.

It is only when I renounce selfish attachments – to things, to creatures, to people – that I can love freely. Without freedom, the relationship is a contract: if you give me one pound of love, I'll give you one pound back. If we keep asking "How much do my parents love me? How much does my partner love me? How much do my children love me?" we will become like King Lear, standing under that dreadful sky and turning to the stars to say, "You see me here, you gods, a poor old man, as full of grief as age, wretched in both."

For those who have reduced their self-will, there is little pain in personal relationships. What others might look upon as an affront or a source of agony is just a little pinprick, not worth worrying about. In fact, it is the mark of those who are selfless to be more concerned about the other person's pain. If they receive a blow, they can shrug it off; but if they see someone else in distress – perhaps somebody who gets upset because they can't have their way – they can say, "Yes, that's how I used to feel before I learned how to be detached. Let me see if I can help."

Those who are detached are wise in relationships because

they can step out of their own shoes and wear the other person's shoes for a moment. They can get their ego out of the way and see situations more clearly. This is much harder than it sounds, because it calls for detachment from ourselves.

We need to free our capacity to love from compulsive attachments not only to people but to things. Every time we get overly involved in material possessions, part of our capacity for love is lost. This is not a plea for poverty; I am talking about attachment. Particularly in a wealthy country, things can simply accumulate. This is how we can all get caught.

When I first came to the U.S. in 1959, I made friends with a welcoming American family in Kansas City. It was an education for all of us. Coming from India, I was astonished that the family had added an additional garage for a new Lincoln Continental. In India in those days, owning a car was only for the very, very few, and a second car was all but unheard of. So I took the liberty of asking my friend why he needed a second car. He was a bit embarrassed, but finally he explained: "In this neighborhood, everybody has a Continental for prestige."

His new garage had electric doors, something I had never seen before. As the car approached, a little contraption would alert the doors to go up automatically. Amazing! I began to enjoy playing with it, and once, when I was spending the weekend with them, he scored off me. When some friends of his dropped by to find out what the "distinguished Indian philosopher" (that was me) had been doing lately, he answered loudly, "The Indian philosopher is playing with the electric garage doors."

We can get fond of electronic devices, cars, homes, any material thing. But it is the nature of material possessions to give us less and less satisfaction the longer we have them. After a while what economists call the law of diminishing returns begins to apply. What we formerly liked not only ceases to be a source of satisfaction; it becomes a source of dissatisfaction, because change and decay are inherent in all our relationships with finite things.

> *Let us live in joy, never hating those who hate*
> *us. Let us live in freedom, without hatred even*
> *among those who hate.* [197]

IT MAY BE easy for me to say I love the people of Iceland, because I don't have any emotional ties with Iceland. If I were teaching at the University of Reykjavík and developed entanglements there, it wouldn't be so easy for me to be on an even keel in that city.

As long as we do not have emotional entanglements, it is easy to be pleasant. When we meet a person for the first time, we can exchange friendly greetings and come home and say, "I met a really nice fellow today." There may be very little to base a judgment upon, but we come home in a good mood.

On the other hand, when you have a son who has to keep up with his peer group and is going in for certain experiments in psychedelics and has affiliations with certain rock bands, the exchange is different. Here is someone who is your flesh and blood going away from all that you stand for. That's the test. If you can keep your mind calm – not agreeing or disagreeing with him – and love him completely, you have passed the test. You are giving him a personal example of living in wisdom, and the gulf between you will be bridged to some extent.

My grandmother used to say that if we withdraw our love and respect from our children, who else will give it to them? She belonged to that simple school of parent-child relationships in which whatever our children do, we have to stand by them. This didn't mean she would connive at behavior she did not approve of, but she would never withdraw her love and respect.

When, out of fear of emotional entanglements, we try to withdraw into ourselves and live in an ivory tower, we are losing an opportunity for spiritual growth. One of the great advantages of family life is that there are so many opportunities for trouble every day. You never know where it is going to come from, which makes you vigilant all the time – and on the spiritual path it is necessary to be alert every moment.

Without strong emotional entanglements, for example, we don't have the opportunity to transform anger into compassion. After all, we are not likely to get upset with the mail carrier, with whom our relationship is probably friendly. It's only with those close to us that we can have ambivalent attitudes. One moment you want to say to your girlfriend, "Don't ever leave me!" and the next moment, "Why don't you?" If you are not emotionally entangled, people cannot upset you.

The curious fact is that our relationships are just the right context for spiritual progress. After all is said and done, these opportunities come to every one of us. It's not just the back-benchers who have difficulties. Everybody has emotional entanglements, but some don't make use of them while others can be inspired by them. It requires a tremendous amount of determination – patient, persistent endeavor – to make use of these occasions for growth.

At home, we have so many opportunities in our relationships – with father or mother, husband or wife, friends and neighbors. It does not matter how strained the bond has been or how agitated we feel – or how agitated they feel – when we are together; we can learn gradually to overcome the damage and repair the relationship. That is the exact context where we can transform whatever agitation we feel into complete love.

Where we do not feel agitated – perhaps because there is no emotional tie – there is not the same opportunity for spiritual development. You may think, "I'm such a secure person in my relationship with the mailman," but you can't grow in such a relationship because it isn't close enough. That is why when people go and live in the forest out of a mistaken idea that this will deepen their spiritual practice, it doesn't usually succeed, because trees can't agitate you. They don't use abusive language or say things to provoke you. Animals may attack you if that is their nature, but not even a king cobra is capable of the vitriolic venom that some people use when they are roused.

> *They think, "These children are mine; this*
> *wealth is mine." They cannot even call*
> *themselves their own, much less their children*
> *or wealth.* [62]

IT IS NOT only the concept of "I" that is a difficult barrier to spiritual awareness. The concept of "mine" is an equally difficult barrier when our love is trapped in just two or three people dear to us. When we have particular attachments to just two or three people, to put it bluntly, we are really in love with annexes of our own ego, and the Buddha would say that there really isn't anything admirable in loving your annex. You're still loving your own building.

If we get attached only to our own, then at the same time we are excluding others – just by virtue of this personal attachment that says only those near to us are worthy of love. A pithy saying in Malayalam catches this perfectly: "To mother crow, her own chick is golden."

I see ravens every day near our road, and if I could speak their language I would ask, "Do you have any little ones?"

"Yes."

"What is their color?"

"Pure gold."

So it is with us human beings: we get attached to what is ours. Therefore, the Buddha is careful to make a distinction between selfless love and the desire to possess others. There is one kind of possessiveness about money and material things, but there is another kind which is even more harmful: trying to possess people in personal relationships. When there is this desire to possess, the relationship is in danger of becoming compulsive, which means we will always lose the other person. In trying to possess anyone, we are actually bringing about our separation from that person. The answer is neither to possess nor to dispossess, but to put the other person first, so that we can get closer and closer.

Take the bond between parents and children. Some time ago a friend told me about the constant turmoil in his relationship with his son. On the one hand, he could not let the boy go and grow up, and in turn his son could not let go of the father and be independent. Both were miserable. They could not live with each other, and they could not live away from each other. This is what the desire to possess can lead to even in a caring parent-child relationship. The parent wants the child to be a child always, and the child is afraid of growing up. This is the taint that causes difficulties: on the one hand to possess and on the other hand to be possessed.

Many of the boys and girls I knew in my village had countless difficulties with their parents because of this lack of detachment. In these homes, they often came together only to agitate and be agitated. In every country, wise parents will know that their children will have to live in different conditions. In a fast-changing society like ours, the world changes even in the span of a generation. So I often tell young people that the best our parents should expect from us is that we should be healthy, secure, and selfless, and grow to our full height, wherever we live, whatever pattern of living we follow. With a certain amount of detachment, wise parents can prepare the children to fly away from the nest and live in the firmament on their own.

The Buddha concludes this verse with a marvelous finale: you do not even belong to yourself. You say you are going to possess this house and that person, but even your body doesn't belong to you. If I say my body belongs to me, the Buddha would retort, "When the great bill collector comes and knocks on the door, can you say, 'This body is mine. I am not going to give it to you'? If that were true, Death would have to say, 'Sorry, wrong address.'" That's the argument. The body has been given to us on a temporary loan so that we can use it for giving a good account of our lives in terms of the selfless service we can render.

If even the body doesn't belong to us, how can we talk about sons and daughters belonging to us? How can we possibly say,

"This is my son, whom I own; this is my daughter, whom I'll never let go"? The Compassionate Buddha says, Leave out this little word "my." It is not only "I" that is the cause of trouble, which is bad enough, but also "my" and "mine."

Pointedly, the Buddha asks us, Don't we love not only our children but everybody's children enough to make sure that they have a fair chance of growing up in a loving world? If we look at our lives – the way we act, the way governments function, the way the mass media operates – it doesn't look as if we care for anything at all. Our lives should show that we care, not only for our children but everybody's children.

In every relationship where there is perfect love, the question of possession never comes up. All of us are capable of this kind of love. Love is inherent in us as human beings. If only we can remove the fog of selfish attachment from our eyes, all of us will be wise in our relationships.

> *If you find a friend who is good, wise, and*
> *loving, walk with him all the way and*
> *overcome all dangers.* [328]

> *It is good to have friends when friendship is*
> *mutual. Good deeds are friends at the time of*
> *death. But best of all is going beyond sorrow.*
> [331]

EVEN THE BUDDHA had to face disharmony and opposition, as we have seen in the stories about Devadatta. Among the Buddha's followers there were more than a few who had a lot of self-will and quarreled a great deal. In the Buddhist scriptures a story is told to show how the Buddha dealt with some troublesome monks. Because the Buddha loved the monks with compassion and detachment, he was able to oppose them gently yet firmly.

At one time, among the monks at Kosambi there were some who got easily resentful, could not overcome jealousy, and in fact were in a bad mood most of the time. Slowly, two leaders spread the bacillus of disharmony to the other monks, until the monastery was divided into two warring camps.

It caused great sorrow to the Compassionate One that anyone professing to follow his teachings should ever waste time in ridiculous quarrels. He tried to persuade them to live in peace, speaking out against disharmony again and again, but when he saw that there were still many who were not responding, he decided to go away to the forest.

The monks tried to dissuade him. "Blessed One, if you go we will be desolate."

"When complete harmony prevails, brothers," he replied, "and everyone is living in accordance with unity and the dharma, I'll come back. But not until then."

Most of the monks were terribly worried about how the Buddha was going to live in the forest. Ananda, who was the Buddha's cousin and his devoted attendant, was inconsolable. But although Ananda was one of the closest, there were others, too, who attended upon the Buddha, and every one of them considered it a great privilege to participate in caring for the person whose life was so precious to all. In spite of all their quarreling and irritability, most of the monks were upset.

Reaching the depths of the forest, the Buddha soon heard the roars of wild animals. It would have been natural to be afraid, but since he was the Buddha, always aware of the unity of life, protective forces surrounded him. So, the chronicles say, an elephant came to the Blessed One, knelt down, raised his trunk, and saluted him with love and respect. Remembering his youth as a prince, when he had learned to ride an elephant, the Buddha knew how to treat an elephant as a friend.

The elephant went away, but in the evening he came back – with a monkey. Knowing the Buddha must be hungry, his new friends brought bunches of bananas, coconuts, and other kinds of fruits and vegetables.

As the sun was about to set, the elephant spread a bed of leaves for the Buddha. Banana, mango, and jack leaves make a comfortable bed, so the Buddha lay down and fell sound asleep while the elephant watched. That night when a tiger passed nearby, the elephant looked hard at the tiger to say, "It's not good for you to come here." The Buddha slept soundly.

In the morning they all went down to the river just like three small boys and had a swim. The elephant showed the Buddha a few tricks, and of course the Buddha knew a few tricks himself. The Compassionate One became just like a little boy, the kind of boy that he had been years ago in Kapilavastu.

So it went for many days: the Buddha, the elephant, and the monkey quite happy and content, just like the three musketeers – one for all and all for one – while the monks in Kosambi were having a miserable time. Finally, the monks realized how much they had grieved the Buddha by their meaningless quarrels. Together they went to the forest, where they were surprised to find the Buddha radiantly happy.

"We understand that we have caused you deep pain," said the monks, "but now we have become aware of our faults and we promise to live in harmony. So won't you come back? It must be a hard life for you here in the wild forest."

The Buddha replied, "Not even Ananda has taken as tender care of me as my friends the elephant and the monkey have. But I will return with you now because the time has come."

Like the Buddha, we can learn to oppose others tenderly if we have detachment. If a self-willed person tries to ride rough-shod over us and we offer no nonviolent resistance, that is a sign that we're not only lacking in loving detachment but also show-ing lack of respect. Particularly in those personal relationships in which we are insecure, this is often what happens: we do feel resentment, but we do not try to oppose tenderly.

None of us are born detached, but through spiritual disci-plines we can learn to be reasonably detached in any situation, which means we can stand back and see the situation clearly and therefore help others to clear their eyes also. Just as a long jumper steps back and takes a running leap, we need to be able to step back from a situation before jumping in, which means we cannot be compulsively involved. If our self-will is out of the way, we will be able to see life clearly. Then we can act wisely and love deeply.

Everyone responds to this kind of unspoken love because in their heart of hearts they know that here is someone they can trust, someone who will stand by them through thick and thin. Without this awareness, most talk of love, sadly, only applies for a limited period.

The person whose ego is not involved is not lacking in love; he or she is capable of even greater love. If someone causes such people problems, that does not affect their love. It is when we are not detached from ourselves that we get upset and move away if someone causes us trouble – or, if we are foolish, even try to cause that person trouble in return.

Now we come to a pressing question: how can we get close to people without getting entangled? I have been asked this question many times. All of us, it seems, know what entanglement is. We know we can get caught in all kinds of situations: entangled with people and mistaking it for love; entangled with things and believing we have found security. Unfortunately, the tendency to get bound like this – to people, to situations, to jobs – can be a very serious obstacle to spiritual growth.

A lot of people even have a flair for entanglement with others. Wherever they go, they must tie a few knots. The way out is for them to put others first. If you can put others first, you will never lose your freedom. It is when you put yourself first that you cannot escape entanglement. You are going to tie knots as long as you keep saying, "How much pleasure can I get? How much attention can I get?" Always ask, "How can I put this person's welfare first?" You'll get fonder and fonder of them, and less and less entangled. That's the secret.

Physical attraction can tie one of the strongest of these knots. Sex has a beautiful place in loving, loyal, lasting relations, but where there is no loyalty, no tenderness, no selflessness, instead of cementing the relationship sex eventually disrupts it. In a relationship that is based on mutual respect, the passage of time draws us closer and closer – and, in addition, removes many of the obstacles to our progress into deeper meditation.

THERE CAN BE no love without giving – of time, of energy, of oneself. And giving means *giving*, not bestowing something in the hope of getting something in return, which is what we commonly understand giving to be for. This is the foundation of business, but it can never be the basis of love. Yet how often we think of love, and romantic relationships, not as occasions for giving but for receiving!

This isn't an observation limited to the Buddha. Jane Austen, whom I enjoyed teaching when I was a professor of English in India, understood this quite clearly. Remember that entertaining scene in *Pride and Prejudice* where Mr. Collins proposes to Elizabeth? My undergraduate students enjoyed performing scenes from favorite English novels, and this is one of the most successful scenes I directed. It was acted by an all-girl cast – no boys allowed – and they were all good actresses, who threw themselves into rehearsals. On the night of the performance we were amazed when over a thousand people came from the town to the campus, where they were accommodated under a large open canopy called a *shamiana*. We knew we owed it to such a receptive audience to put on the best performance possible.

Now the scene is set. First there is Elizabeth – young, beautiful, and as independent as you can get anywhere in any country in any age. Then there is Mr. Collins – not so young, not so beautiful, and as silly as you can get in any country in any age. Mr. Collins enters with all his egocentric dignity, with no thought of anybody else, completely preoccupied with his own thoughts: "I must be satisfied; I must be happy . . ." He cannot even imagine he will fail to impress Elizabeth. The thought is alien to him.

Elizabeth greets him politely. He makes his proposal, and with all the grace she can muster she says, "I do not deserve this honor."

He replies, "Please reconsider, my dear. Do not keep me waiting."

Elizabeth is edging towards the doorway but finds the way to retreat cut off. So she plays for time. "To what do I owe this great honor?"

This serious, grown-up man says, "My patroness Lady Catharine de Bourgh wants me to marry."

At this point the whole shamiana is shaking with laughter, and it looks like the canopy might fall down. Just imagine, you propose to someone by saying that your uncle has just come from Chicago and he insists that you marry her! It may not be subtle, but it certainly went down very well with our audience.

Then came a line that no doubt escaped all but a few. Collins says, "I am sure you will make me the best wife."

Elizabeth's quizzical glance needs no words. "I don't think you will make me the best husband." The actress, a very talented young woman, showed her meaning just by her glance – just by raising her eyebrows and giving us a smile.

In personal relationships, whether in India or England or America, this is what leads to trouble: "How much can you give me? How happy can you make me?" Even this episode with Mr. Collins and Elizabeth is a commentary on how most of us are inclined to try to use the other person. As a corrective against this universal human failing we can put the other person first.

Imagine rewriting Mr. Collins's lines. He could come to Elizabeth and say, "I would try to do everything possible to ensure your happiness by turning my back every day upon my opinions and upon what Lady Catharine de Bourgh has got to say." There is little doubt that things would have turned out differently. Who knows? He might have been stuck with Elizabeth for life. Because that is the way to win anyone's heart: putting that person first and oneself last.

> *Give up anger, give up pride, and free yourself*
> *from worldly bondage. No sorrow can befall*
> *those who never try to possess people and*
> *things as their own.* [221]

WHEREVER THERE IS an inability to put the other person first, anger will follow, for separateness and anger are close companions. Lamentably, the main thrust of our modern conditioning seems to keep anger burning, to maintain resentments and hostilities at their most furious level, often under the impression that to do otherwise stifles our personality.

The Buddha says simply, "Give up anger." This is his direct method of teaching. He is not suggesting that we reduce our anger or give in to it only on special occasions. He says, "Give it up." Even righteous indignation is not permitted. On certain occasions, we may feel that principled fury should be permitted, even applauded, but the Buddha rules this out too, because it can only increase our separateness and lead us finally to despair.

War and violence in any form are not compatible with the way of the Buddha, who often spoke about the suffering caused by war and the utter failure of violence to solve conflicts. In India we learn as children the Sanskrit proverb *ahimsa paramo dharma*: never to injure anyone under any circumstances is considered to be the highest dharma, the highest mark of human evolution.

> *Long is the night to those who are awake; long is the road to those who are weary. Long is the cycle of birth and death to those who know not the dharma.* [60]

WHATEVER LEADS TO the unity of life is dharma; whatever violates that unity is *adharma*, "not dharma." Jealousy, competition, greed, anger, fear, and lust are all violations of dharma that lead away from health, happiness, security, love, and wisdom.

Once a householder asked the Compassionate Buddha, "What is the proof that we are one?"

"When you hate someone, it is you who will suffer – sometimes mentally, sometimes even physically," he replied. "When you love someone more than you love yourself, you become well."

This is the simplest proof that spiritually we are one. When I love others more than I love myself, I become strong, secure, wise, beautiful. When I live for myself, for my own profit and pleasure, I die little by little, wasting my precious birthright as a human being. When I live for my parents, my partner, my children, my friends, I grow in love, wisdom, security, and the capacity for selfless service.

Those who have learned to forget themselves in the welfare of all live in accordance with dharma. They may never have been to a university, may not even know how to read or write, but wherever they live, they will be a force for good, a force for peace. Wherever they go, others will respond naturally and deeply to them.

Even in the academic world in which I lived for many years, I knew colleagues who were more impressed not by scholarship alone but by those professors who thought more about what they could give to their students and their community than about how much money they could get or what prerogatives they could demand from the university. Those who lead such selfless lives don't ask how much they can get but how much they can give.

In so far as we live only for ourselves, we deprive the world of our small contribution. When we lead a life of personal pursuits, the Buddha doesn't deny that it's enjoyable personally. He doesn't deny that it can bring rewards. Yet the more thoughtful, sensitive person will feel uncomfortable if he or she cannot make some contribution every day to the world in which they live. This is what dharma means, and it doesn't require any special spiritual awareness to understand it.

We know that people who are preoccupied with themselves, who always seem to try to take personal advantage at the expense of others, become a disturbing influence wherever they go. The Compassionate Buddha would not call such people wicked; they simply do not understand what he calls "the good, true law": that all of life is an indivisible unity.

Life becomes a burden for those who believe "I am separate;

therefore, I can manipulate you. You are separate; therefore, I expect you to manipulate me." In those who follow the path of adharma, consciousness becomes more and more restricted by separateness. When this tendency becomes most extreme, they are driven to isolate and estrange themselves from others more and more. The tragic consequence is hostility and suspicion. "I don't want to be David. I don't want to be Bert. I want to be me." That is the voice of separateness. In saying that I want to be me, I am pushing Bert and David out, further and further away.

> *Don't try to build your happiness on the*
> *unhappiness of others. You will be enmeshed in*
> *a net of hatred.* [291]

THE BUDDHA STARTED this line of reasoning by tickling us with a feather, then prodding us with a little twig. Now, finally, he hits us with a stick. Separateness, he says, is a malady to which all human beings are subject to some extent, but when it gets inflated, it makes life miserable. It's not lack of money or lack of prestige that makes life miserable; it is an inflated ego. In other words, loss of selfishness is not a loss but the greatest possible gain, and selflessness the greatest source of happiness.

The Buddha enunciates this quite clearly: anyone who tries to build his or her happiness on the suffering of others is doomed to misery. He is not making a conjecture. He says this is a law, the law of karma. When others do not behave as we expect and we avoid them or are curt to them, it is we who are going into prison – the prison of separateness. When we dislike others, the Buddha would say, that is just the time to move closer to them;

otherwise it is we who are going to be "enmeshed in a net of hatred."

Tragically, once we are caught in this net we no longer see people and situations clearly. We no longer know what is real and what is not, so it becomes almost impossible to come out of the prison of the ego. We have entered a hall of mirrors where everyone looks not only separate but distorted.

When I was growing up, the circus toured even the remotest areas of Kerala, and the hall of mirrors was a favorite amusement for us village boys. We paid a penny to go inside a big tent to see ourselves looking first like Chesterton – well-fed and rotund – and then in the next mirror like Shaw, tall and rail-thin. In the next mirror our head might disappear; in the next our legs. Somehow we found this a source of amusement, because we knew that once we went outside we would still be well-proportioned and attractive. We knew we weren't really like the creature in the funhouse, and we knew that no one else was like that either.

When we are angry or overcome by hatred, however, we are in the ego's hall of mirrors, and we don't know it at all. Everywhere we see distortions – ugly, selfish, evil – and we ourselves are included as well as others. Fortunately, the Buddha says, we can come out of this house of horrors once and for all: give our ticket back to the ringmaster and say, "You're welcome to keep it. I know now that nobody is really like that."

ALL RELIGIONS, BUDDHISM included, address our need to return to our original wholeness, our native state of self-lessness. In Hinduism as well as Buddhism, it is said that we have forgotten this essential unity simply through ignorance. "Fallen" sounds like something we have done deliberately. "Forgetting" is much more compassionate, much more dignified, because it enables us to save face and just say, "I forgot."

The goal in all religions is the same, the disciplines are the same, but the teaching is couched in the language of the day, using the phrases and rhetoric prevalent at the time. The differences are in the mode of expression; in the mode of experience there is no difference at all. So Buddhism explains this ignorance of unity using a distinctive philosophical style. It offers the doctrine of "not self" and the principle of "dependent origination" not for the purpose of creating theories, but for the very practical purpose of helping us return to our state of original oneness.

The principle of dependent origination – also called the chain of causation – is usually said to consist of twelve links, but on occasion we will see ten links or even nine. Sometimes the image of an ever-rotating wheel is used, with twelve spokes. It may be thought of as the wheel of the mind, or it may be thought of as the wheel of the universe. What is important is not the number of links or spokes but to be able to understand the Buddha's terse equation: "This arising, that arises. Therefore, this not arising, that does not arise." Ignorance arising, separateness arises – by a chain of causal links. When ignorance is dispelled, separateness vanishes.

Everything, the Buddha says, exists with reference to something else. Nothing is independent; everything is interdependent. If I were to tell Albert Einstein, "My friend Stuart has moved," Einstein would reply that my statement is incomplete. "Everything moves with reference to something else," he would say, "so please complete your statement: Stuart has moved with reference to Bob."

Actually, the Buddha would add, Stuart really doesn't even exist separately from Bob. Both are a part of the same whole; it is an illusion that they exist apart from that whole. If we examine the wheel of dependent origination closely, we will see it tells us that no person, no thing, exists separately, apart from every other person and thing. So even to say that Stuart is a different person from Bob is a distortion of reality, because the distinction between the "self" that is Stuart – or, more precisely, that Stuart thinks he is – and everything else is more a convention than a reality.

The reality is unity, but as long as the delusion of separateness exists, the cycle of birth and death continues. The wheel continues to turn. Therefore, just as the good physician tries to help the patient by showing him how his disease has been caused, Buddha the diagnostician asks, what is the first cause that makes all the rest of the pain follow?

Again, in Hinduism as well as Buddhism, the answer is *avidya*: utter ignorance. A man may be a great scientist, a woman may be a great poet, and yet know nothing about life. This may sound like a condemnation, but there is a promise behind it. Just as ignorant people can be educated, a selfish person – a spiritually ignorant person – can be educated too.

Avidya means literally "not knowing," so naturally we ask,

"Not knowing what?" Every sage who has reached the other shore will say it means not knowing that you and I are one. That is the first link in the chain, the link that leads finally – in an interdependent, interconnected manner – to the last link of old-age-and-death. From the first link, all the rest follows: with avidya, all the forces of separateness come into play.

The full chain is: ignorance, samskaras, I-consciousness, name-and-form, senses, sense-contact, sensation, craving, clinging, becoming, birth, and old-age-and-death. In contemporary language, forgetfulness of unity conditions the will to separateness, which leads to I-consciousness. As the will to separateness gets stronger, the sense of "I" becomes more pronounced and self-will becomes fiercer. And the moment the switch of self-will is thrown, all kinds of disruptive forces are let loose. It's not necessary to throw every little switch – of anger, resentment, hostility, malice, jealousy, and so on. Once self-will is switched on, everything else is turned on automatically. This is a hair trigger; one touch and all the undesirable negative forces begin to work. That's what the terse formula "this arising, that arises" means: the moment self-will is allowed to rise, it will naturally increase, regularly get inflated, and then everything begins to go wrong. Ultimately, relationships will not endure; estrangements will come between even those who have been close.

Because everything is connected, the Buddha says, we can't work on each little switch one by one. There are thousands of little switches! We can't spend our lives working on one after the other: ten years for removing jealousy, another ten years for removing insecurity. Life isn't long enough for a piecemeal approach. The Buddha says, Get hold of the main switch! Reduce self-will. Yes, it is very difficult, but it can be done.

THERE IS ANOTHER way to understand avidya: ignorance means we have become trapped in this short little span of one lifetime, utterly unmindful of the vast seas of time that stretch on either side. There are millions and millions of years extending before we came into this life. There are millions and millions of years continuing after we pass out from this life. Avidya and all the other spokes in the wheel tell the story of how we came to forget that this life is not all there is.

Imagine going to a movie theater and getting utterly absorbed in the movie, which is full of drama – birth and death, triumph and defeat, love and war. You get so interested that you stay and watch it again and again and again. Gradually you forget there is any world outside the theater. You forget that you have to go home, that you have to go to work; you just stay on in the theater. You even sleep there, and when you get hungry you go to the snack bar and have popcorn. The theater, with that particular show, has become your world.

The Buddha says that is our condition. We have all forgotten we have a home, forgotten that we are free to go home; we are caught in the ever-turning wheel of birth and death. In nirvana we don't learn anything new: we remember. We return to the original state before avidya, the Garden of Eden we have forgotten.

The Buddha never indulges in speculation, never goes in for

philosophy for its own sake. The only reason he has given us the principle of dependent origination is to help us understand the nature of life and put it in practical perspective. It is because we know nothing about the nature of life that we suffer more than necessary. Because we do not know what life is really like, we make foolish demands, and these demands bind us more and more tightly to the ever-turning wheel. We become unhappy, frustrated, and bitter, and go about nursing grievances against others – all because we do not understand that "When this arises, that arises."

On the other hand, "Where that does not exist, this does not exist." That's the whole course, you see: "With the cessation of that comes the cessation of this. With the cessation of self-will comes the cessation of suffering." This is the sum and substance of dependent origination. The class is over, and we can go home.

This is a severe diagnosis, but there is a cure: the practice of meditation. When we go deep in meditation, the blind self-will of which the Buddha speaks will fall away, and with it the whole chain of causation. Then we see reality as it is, beyond the realm of dependent origination, free from sorrow and death.

After this supreme discovery, most mystics look back upon the long travail of their past lives with compassion, even as a kind of comedy. They will say, "See how stupid I was in being resentful and hostile, in manipulating others and living for myself!" It is not the immorality that strikes them; it is the utter stupidity of it. That's why some mystics call this world a game.

Let us live in joy, never attached among
those who are selfishly attached. Let us live in
freedom even among those who are bound by
selfish attachments.

Let us live in joy, never hoarding things among
those who hoard. Let us live in growing joy like
the bright gods. [199–200]

PASSIONATELY IN LOVE with each other, the chronicles say, Prince Siddhartha and Princess Yashodhara had been
together for many lives. Their devotion to one another is the
supreme example not of selfish attachment but of selfless love.
The Jataka stories tell how in former lives, when the Buddha was
a tiger, Yashodhara was a tigress; when he was king of the deer,
she was the queen. In life after life they came together, and so it
was not chance that when the Buddha-to-be was born as a
prince in the kingdom of the Shakyas, Yashodhara was born a
princess in a kingdom nearby.

When it came time for the young princess to marry, following the custom of the warrior clans, she was allowed to choose
her husband from among the eligible young men in neighbor-
ing realms. When Yashodhara came forward to make her choice,
Siddhartha's face lit up as if illumined by a lamp. His smile was
one of recognition, because they had lived and loved many
times in many lives before. He confidently passed all the tests
that were set to prove his love for her, and in due course they
were married.

When the prince went to the forest, Yashodhara longed for
him day after day. Hearing that he was now sleeping on the

ground, she left her soft bed and slept on the floor. Hearing that he was fasting, she too fasted. Like the warrior princess she was, Yashodhara faced her separation with courage and dedicated her life to caring for their young son, Rahula.

After years of separation, when Siddhartha returned to Kapilavastu as the Compassionate Buddha, he came to give his family the wisdom of the dharma. He had left as a tormented young man determined to find the answer to the riddle of impermanence and death, leaving behind even his wife and child to practice meditation on the slopes of the Himalayas. Now, as he walked along the main street of his old city, people crowded around to look upon him in wonder.

Yashodhara gazed at him from the balcony of the palace and saw a royal sage who had renounced the world and attained nirvana. Her friends said, "The prince is passing by. Quickly, you must go down and see him before he is gone!"

Yashodhara replied, "If I really love him with no thought of myself, he will come to me."

"He's a monk," they tell her. "He cannot come into anyone's home." Absolutely confident, Yashodhara insisted that he was sure to come up to her apartments to see her, whether monastic rules forbid it or not. "The power of my love will draw him to me. He will come up to see me."

And just as she said, when the Buddha passed in front of the palace he stopped and told his disciples, "Please excuse me for a while. I will go and see my family."

You can almost hear the murmurs of the crowd. "Is he breaking his vow? Isn't he a monk?"

But the Buddha goes up, and Yashodhara is overwhelmed with joy. She who had suffered a great loss now sees the Buddha's eyes pouring love on all, his wisdom pouring balm on the wounds of all, and she realizes that her loss has been the gain of the whole world. All her pain dies in that realization, for she knows in her heart that she is included in his great love, and that in her renunciation she has freed the Buddha to fulfill himself as the savior of all.

She turns to Rahula and says, "This is your father."

Looking at the face radiating love, little Rahula asks, "That's my father?"

"Yes, he is now a light unto the whole world. Go and ask him for your legacy."

It is one of the great scenes in the life of the Buddha when he accepts his son as his disciple and welcomes him into the order.

Yashodhara was a great soul who, like the Buddha himself, was destined to attain complete freedom in that very life. Casting aside her royal station, she became a nun and in due time, free of all fetters, entered into the peace of nirvana.

This story is to remind us that there have been figures like the Buddha and Yashodhara who in their personal lives have given us an inspiring example we too can follow to the small extent that it is possible for ordinary people like us. We are not asked to enter into the monastic life. It is enough if we begin from today onwards to expand our love rather than confine it to two or three people who are dear to us. At home, at work, in trying to forget ourselves in augmenting the welfare of those around us, we can gradually extend our loving concern to our society and the wider world. Every day, if we try to think more about others even when it is at our personal expense, we have found the best path – the right path for all.

◇ *Traveling Light*

ON THE NIGHT of his enlightenment the Buddha made the profound discovery that nothing happens by chance – not because events are predestined, but because every act, every word, every thought is connected by cause and effect. What we do, say, and even think has consequences. Words and thoughts are included, for they cause things to happen. What we say and think has consequences for the world around us, for they condition how we act.

This is what Hinduism and Buddhism call the law of karma. Karma means something done, whether as cause or as effect. Actions in harmony with dharma bring good karma and add to health and happiness. Selfish actions, at odds with dharma, bring unfavorable karma and pain. Instead of trapping us in a fatalistic snare, this gives us freedom. Because we alone have brought ourselves into this state, we ourselves, by working hard, can reach the supreme state which is nirvana.

In order to cross the river of life, we have to undergo all the necessary spiritual disciplines, but it is equally important to undo our unfavorable karma. There is a very close correspondence between the pace at which we are able to work out our karma and the pace at which we make progress on the spiritual path. Nirvana comes when all the karma has been worked out, not before. When all the debts of karma have been paid, it means that our mind is still. Then all the fetters of karma have at last been released, and we are not capable of accumulating more karma.

The Buddha does have compassion, infinite compassion, but he knows that we will not be able to make the journey to nirvana if we are not heroes: if we don't take a good look at our situation in order to meet our personal karma and overcome it. No one is condemned to a life of misery. Little by little we can lighten the load of our karma. That is the important point. It is not fate, it is not the stars, it is we ourselves who are in control of our own lives.

We begin by reducing our cargo. Long-distance hikers know they have to reduce what they carry to the minimum. It is the same with spiritual travelers. How can we make progress towards nirvana if we are adding more and more to the burden we carry on our backs? So the Buddha gives us the secret in a pithy verse: don't add to your karma by striking at others. It will only bring you suffering and prevent any progress on the spiritual path.

> *If, hoping to be happy, you strike at others who*
> *also seek happiness, you will be happy neither*
> *here nor hereafter.*
>
> *If, hoping to be happy, you do not strike at*
> *others who are also seeking happiness, you will*
> *be happy here and hereafter.* [131–132]

IN THESE VERSES the Buddha uses a homely word, *danda*, which means a big stick. He says that if John takes up a stick and hits Jack, Jack is going to hit John back. Then John is going to hit Jack back harder. Finally, both Jack and John will become more and more estranged, more and more separate, more and more hurt. This is the law of karma put in the frankest language: whatever injury you do to others has to come back to you – and whatever good you do has to come back to you too.

Isn't there an Australian tool called a boomerang? If you throw it, it will come back to you. Try it; you can see for yourself how it will come back to you. Words and deeds can become boomerangs if we throw them at others to hurt them. They are going to come round and strike us.

We don't see the connection because there is a time lag – and because there are so many boomerangs in the air. We are preoccupied with so many innumerable things, have thrown so many boomerangs and are getting hit on so many sides – there, here, everywhere – that we don't know which hit is being returned. If we could use a cosmic computer, the kind that appears in science fiction films, no doubt the law of karma could be verified. But imagine the complexity of it! There are billions of people on the face of the earth, and each has got to be given the exact place in accordance with previous karma. A computer magnified a billion billion billion times is required to put all these endless bits of karma together so that we are born in the right context to enjoy the fruits of our assets and pay the price of our liabilities.

If you could program a karmic computer correctly, you would be able to match the hits. The computer could tell you that a particular hit was given to you by Alice in return for the hit that you gave Ellen. When you said something to Ellen that day at the swimming pool, the computer kept a record of it. Later, when you hear the very same words from Alice at the movie theater, the computer makes the match. No one has this kind of science-fiction computer, but it is still possible, with practice and insight, to begin to connect events – and when we do, we will agree that, yes, that is how the law of karma works.

Karma may mystify us, I agree. It may seem unreasonable. But it can be explained in direct, contemporary language. For example, the law of karma says that if I am impolite to my parents, I will have children who are impolite to me. My children observe the way I conduct myself to my parents, and that is what they learn. As my children observe my attitude towards my parents, they are learning to conduct themselves in exactly the same way towards me. When I respect my parents, my children will learn how to respect me. It is so simple – and yet not simple at all.

Refrain from evil deeds, which cause suffering
later. Perform good deeds, which can cause no
suffering. [314]

THOSE WHO CAN learn easily, who commit a few mistakes
and then understand, hardly meet with sorrow later. They find
that their burden of karma gets lighter and lighter as they move
through life. After committing a few mistakes, they say, "No, no,
no, we don't want to commit these mistakes again and suffer."
This is where sensitive people ask, "Why can't we move in the
right direction simply under persuasion? Why do we have to
have difficulties and deprivations brought upon us in order to
learn? We can change our habits now."

Because only a fully enlightened mind can truly understand
the web of karma, to an extent we must take it on the faith we
place in the Buddha's teaching. But we needn't take it on faith
alone, because much of what the Buddha says can be understood through reason, and certainly we can understand karma
through reason, at least in part. We can begin by accepting that
karma is a benevolent force, intended not to punish but to edu-
cate, so that we can fulfill our purpose in life.

In a great flash of scientific observation, the Buddha discovered that cause and effect are not different. The result of an
action is not separate from the act itself. Cause, passing through
the tunnel of time, becomes effect, but the result is already contained in the cause. Therefore, right effort must produce a right
result – and wrong effort will produce a wrong result.

In our Indian traditions, both Hindu and Buddhist, we have
many, many stories to remind us that the result is contained in

the cause – stories meant to inspire us never to bring harm to anyone. The vast epics of India, the *Ramayana* and the *Mahabharata,* are based on the give and take, thrust and parry, of the law of karma as it works itself out on an immense scale.

The *Ramayana,* which is about Rama, a hero and divine incarnation known all over India, contains many lessons about the law of karma. Dasharatha, a great king, is Rama's father, and even though Dasaratha is beloved in his kingdom for living a selfless life, he dies of a broken heart when Rama goes into the forest in exile.

When I was a young boy I used to ask my granny the kind of question all sensitive people in India ask, "Why should this happen to Rama's father, who was a good man?"

Granny, who could not read or write, knew the *Ramayana* better than anyone else in our family, because almost every day she listened to our village pundit read from the scriptures and comment on them. She narrated Dasharatha's story to me from memory. As a young prince, Dasharatha had gone hunting – grievously enough – in quest of an elephant. Perhaps the elephant had damaged the crops of the villagers, in which case perhaps Dasharatha could have told the villagers to fence the fields. But instead, early in the morning, young Dasharatha went to the river to lie in wait for the elephant that was sure to come to drink.

Soon he heard a rumbling sound, the unmistakable splash of an elephant drinking and playing in the water. Unerringly, he shot his arrow toward the sound, only to discover to his horror that it was a young boy who had been filling a big clay vessel with water. Stricken with remorse, Dasharatha rushed to the father of the dead boy, fell at his feet, and asked for pardon. The father, a sage living in the forest, said, "I give you pardon gladly. I am not capable of anger. But I cannot stop the law of karma. Just as you have broken my heart by killing my only son, your heart will be broken when your son leaves you."

It is a hard story for a child's ears, but that is how my granny taught me to never bring harm to others, even carelessly or unintentionally. She would always explain, "When you help people, you bring joy into your own life; when you hurt people, you bring sorrow. When you support people, you bring happiness; when you attack people, you bring grief." Then she added that Dasharatha saw a vision of Rama as he was dying and passed away joyfully.

My granny planted the seeds of this wisdom when I was a child, but it was only many years later that I began to see the patterns in my own life – how the mistakes I committed, often unwittingly, came back to me. Slowly, I began to understand that these events were not accidents. I was like most people, for whom this wisdom comes only after we have a great deal of experience behind us.

It is only through careful, mature observation that this understanding comes to us: that we can't do harmful things and escape the consequences under any circumstances. When that becomes part of your faith, as it has become mine, you will never do anything harmful, whatever the provocation. Once you come to believe that this is a law, something in you will protect you from harming others – and something in you will inspire you to help others, even at a cost to yourself.

As fresh milk needs time to curdle, a selfish
deed takes time to bring sorrow in its wake.
Like fire smoldering under the ashes, slowly
does it burn the immature. [71]

THE PATTERNS OF karma in our lives usually develop not in one dramatic cataclysm but little by little. Take relationships, for example. Most loving relationships do not grow unloving overnight, but all of us are capable of being unkind. If allowed to grow, little by little this seed of unkindness damages our feelings for each other. Today at breakfast you yield to a little irritation and use harsh language, but after you go to the office everything is fine, so you don't pay any attention to the little incident at breakfast. "Oh," you think, "I got up on the wrong side of the bed, but things are all right now."

Then the next morning it happens again, but instead of getting concerned again you think, "It's such a small thing. We were out of coffee, and I made a silly remark. No one would make an issue out of it." You can easily justify your blunt words. After all, you were being factual. Any reasonable person can see that. You didn't mean to attack anyone; you were just making a statement about the coffee. No one should take it personally.

Then one morning you burn your toast. Someone has set the toaster on high, and the bread pops up smoking like a cinder. You lose your temper. But this time it is your partner who has got up on the wrong side of the bed, and she lets you have it in return. With barely controlled outrage, she informs you that you are the one who always sets the toaster on high, though she has reminded you several times that it will burn the toast. Gradually, the conversation gets more and more heated. One thing leads to another until there is smoke rising in clouds over the breakfast table. The ashes are smoldering, fed by little irritations that are so small we may not even be aware of them. If we are aware, we disregard them as the minor frustrations of daily life. "Oh, it's just the give and take of life. I can take a few pinpricks."

But at the rate of ten pinpricks a day, by the end of the year you have absorbed 3,650 jabs and are beginning to feel like a pincushion. After a few years, your nervous system begins to show the effects. Formerly, if your partner said something that you didn't like, you quietly offered a wry smile. When something tried your patience, you made a joke or even quoted a line from Shakespeare. Now you cannot control your tongue. You cannot help retaliating. Your capacity for tolerance has come to an end, and when that happens not even the best among us, who take pride in having the finest manners, can refrain from saying and doing things we will later regret. It is not because we are bad, but because the ashes have been smoldering for a long time and finally the flames burst out.

> *Let no one think lightly of evil and say to*
> *himself, "Sorrow will not come to me." Little by*
> *little a person becomes evil, as a pot is filled by*
> *drops of water.*
>
> *Let no one think lightly of good and say to*
> *himself, "Joy will not come to me." Little by*
> *little a person becomes good, as a pot is filled*
> *by drops of water.* [121–122]

DROP BY DROP – this is how estrangements start. At the same time, it is by remembering the many good things that happen every day that we strengthen our love and heal our lives. When there is a harsh word, we can remember how many kind words there have been in the past. When there is a thoughtless action, we can remember how much consideration there has been in the past. This restores our sense of proportion.

The observations of one life, no matter how penetrating, cannot be enough to explain the working out of the law of karma, because one life is like a single chapter in a book. It does not tell the whole story. Unlike the Buddha, we do not see the incalculable cycles of birth and death in which the cause and effect of karma is played out as we make the long, long journey to nirvana. But just because we do not see the connections, we should not say that these connections do not exist.

Why should an innocent person suffer? All of us must have asked this question many, many times. Everywhere, every day, blameless people suffer, and we ask, "Why should this have come to her? She hurt no one, offended no one." It is only an illumined Buddha who can answer these questions, because he sees life whole. He sees past, present, and future as part of one living chain, so he can see an infinite procession of cause and effect.

The Buddha would say compassionately, "You see only one brief flash that you call life. There is much more to life than that. If you could see the whole vast saga of evolution, all the things done, said, and thought in the past that come to bear on the present life, you would see an almost infinite web of cause and effect." This attitude is not fatalistic. Rather, it allows us to assume responsibility for our own lives.

During my academic career I read many books by both Indian and Western scholars on the concept of reincarnation, but few of them brought out its utterly practical value, which lies in the choice it offers us to take command of our lives completely and remodel our character, conduct, and consciousness so that we go from birth to birth to a higher level until we attain the ultimate goal of nirvana. A desire to speculate about past lives is a fairly harmless pastime, but much more important than speculating about past lives is to understand the principle of reincarnation, which tells us that our evolution is entirely in our own hands. I can go into a better context in my next life by traveling swiftly, lightly, in this life.

AT THE TIME of death, there is a residue in our deepest consciousness of all that we have thought and spoken and done, all that we have longed for and fought for and schemed for. It's an immense library, and the Buddha says that what is recorded in this library will dictate our next life. It will be the decisive factor in where we are going to be born, in what kind of body, with what kind of mind. Those who have lightened their load of karma in this life will make even more progress towards the goal of nirvana in the next life.

In some schools of Buddhism, the library of karma is called "store-consciousness." You have a little stock at the end of every life, a little parcel of certain tendencies which you have cultivated in that life – ten pounds of anger, ten pounds of fear, and twenty-five pounds of greed, and a few precious jewels of earnestness, courage, and selflessness. It is all kept in the storehouse, and you take it with you into your next life.

Years ago I went to the bus depot to meet a friend, and while I was waiting I was looking about the vast room, where many people were seated passing the time until their buses arrived. It was a very interesting scene. There were people of all types seated on the benches – old, young, men, women, children. And there was a constant stream of buses arriving and leaving.

People were waiting – patiently or impatiently – to hear their particular bus called. "Reno! Reno! The bus for Reno is leaving at Gate 3," came over the public address system, and many stood up, but not everyone. Some were waiting for the Los Angeles bus, and some were going as far as Denver.

People were coming and going, arriving and departing. It reminded me of a scene in the *Tibetan Book of the Dead* in which the state between lives is described. This in-between state is called *bardo*, and we can think of it as a place very much like a bus station – a lively scene which we all will visit eventually. Between two lives, according to this exposition, there is a waiting period because we have to get the right context for rebirth. If we have lacked respect for our parents, we have to wait in bardo until we can be born in a situation where we are likely to have children who will show us the same lack of respect. There is no mystery about this. There is nothing vindictive. It is simply a natural law. We can't blame any outside force or fate and complain, "Why do I have to have children who don't respect me?"

In bardo, in other words, we have to wait for the right bus. We can't take just any bus. If the bus for Reno arrives first, we don't get on it; we wait for the bus for Los Angeles. So there is a precision about the next life. We have to have a son who drops out of school to be a full-time surfer and a daughter who spends her life skiing, and a third child who goes to Mexico and learns to make pottery. It's not easy to get this combination of surfer, skier, and potter. Not many places offer this unusual combination. India is ruled out; Africa is ruled out. Slowly we narrow the field. Which state has cities with both snow-clad mountains and good surf right at hand, and Mexico just a day's drive away? By elimination, it dawns on us: California!

In this cosmic waiting room, only people with a certain kind of karma will take a particular bus. Those who have gambling karma will immediately jump up to take the Reno bus. They tell the other passengers they have a system. "Stick with me, and we'll break the bank." And the others will listen, because everyone with gambling karma will be on that particular bus as it pulls out of the bardo station. Similarly, there is a special bus for people with aggression karma, anxiety karma, greed karma; all get born into times and circumstances that will bring this karma into play.

And good karma too. Every packet of karma is carefully stored. Those who have practiced spiritual disciplines in this life will take that packet with them into the next life. They will be born into a family with good parents who will help them to resume their spiritual journey. It is a great blessing to be born into such a home, where we can just take up our journey where we left off.

> *Better than ruling this world, better than*
> *attaining the realm of the gods, better than*
> *being lord of all the worlds, is one step taken*
> *on the path to nirvana.* [178]

MANY MAJOR RELIGIONS teach that after death we can achieve a heavenly world, free from sorrow. According to the

Buddha and the Upanishads, the only difference between heaven and earth is this: on earth, pain and pleasure are mixed. In heaven there is pleasure without pain, which explains why heaven is such a timeless attraction.

According to the law of karma, some will find their way there. They want to have unending pleasure, they don't want to have any pain, and through their good deeds they attain the heavenly state. They don't want to see others suffering because they would feel compelled to try to relieve that suffering. They don't want to come in contact with sorrow or grief. They want to meet with only what is happy, blissful, and joyful. According to Hindu and Buddhist mysticism, these heavenly creatures are called *devas*. Yet the Buddha and the Upanishads may shock us when they question the appeal of heaven, which they say is only for those who are less than enlightened. For those who want nirvana, heaven is a side road.

The Buddha has some fun at the devas' expense, because the heavenly state is not permanent. After they have exhausted all their good karma – after a thousand years, or five thousand years – a kind of heavenly bouncer appears. He says, "It is time for you to go. I must throw you out."

The deva objects, "You can't throw me out. Heaven is my home."

"Your time is up. You have to go back to earth."

In Buddhism and Hinduism, the earth is called the place of work, the place of karma. It is the place where we learn to wake up, the place where we balance our karma books once and for all.

According to the Buddha, devas don't like ordinary people like us attaining illumination. The devas are like the Olympian gods in ancient Greece, who were fond of entertainment, and the human comedy was a source of infinite diversion for them. On their Olympian heights they watch and see a poor man become rich. Then a crash comes. Everybody loses money, including the poor man. Zeus or Athena or Aphrodite says, "Just look at that fellow. He spent forty years making money and now he doesn't have enough to buy a toothbrush!" This is considered high entertainment on Olympus.

The Buddha explains why the gods may show such ill will: he says that though they will never admit it, the gods are jealous. The devas can never attain illumination without returning again to the world of earth. So they are envious when they see any man or woman who is making good progress towards the goal.

In the Hindu and the Buddhist traditions reincarnation is simply taken for granted. It's not a philosophical concept. It's taken for granted that until I become aware that all life is one – until I reach nirvana – I will keep coming back. We will never die; we are eternal. The house in which we live has been demolished and rebuilt many, many times, but we don't die.

The simple truth taught by reincarnation is that until we wake up, we are going to go back to school every fall. There is no end to the number of times we can repeat a grade. We have been registered permanently, so we don't have to register again by mail. We don't have to queue up and seek admission. We are permanent students. Our name is on the rolls. It has been there for a million years, and it's going to be for a million years more if we don't take our education into our own hands.

Here the Buddha is supremely practical. Instead of dwelling on the past and feeling dejected about our karmic ledger, he says, why not begin adding entries to the credit side? Eventually, when the cosmic public accountant – CPA – comes and asks to see the ledger, you can give it to him with confidence. He will look at the debit side first, and of course he will say it's horrible. All you can do is agree. It doesn't help to tear your hair and say, "I wish I'd never been born!" Just agree with him. "Yes, it is awful, even horrible," you say, "but would your honor kindly turn to the other page."

This is the practicality of the Buddha. When the cosmic accountant sees all the entries you have been making on the credit page, even small entries in the margin – a few, you admit, at the last moment – he will say, "Wow! Credit after credit after credit. You have been writing between the lines, in the margins, at the bottom to get them all in." If the debits and credits still don't balance, he may even give you a longer life to go back and add more to the credit side.

> *Conquer anger through gentleness, unkindness*
> *through kindness, greed through generosity,*
> *and falsehood by truth.* [223]

MANY LEGENDS ARE told in the Buddhist scriptures of rich gifts given to the Buddha by kings and merchants, peasants and widows, thieves and prostitutes, rich and poor, who all gained a substantial entry on their karmic accounts because of their loving generosity. King Bimbisara of Magadha was an especially generous giver and sincere follower of the Buddha.

Bimbisara, you may recall, first encountered young Prince Siddhartha when he was on his way to the forest. When the king couldn't persuade the young man to give up his quest, he asked that he return as soon as he had found what he was looking for.

So in the first year after his enlightenment, the Buddha returned again to Rajagaha, where he received a royal welcome from the king.

Now, Rajagaha had a beautiful park called the Bamboo Grove, a wonderful pleasure garden that belonged to the king alone. Every day the king enjoyed resting in the garden, but he fell so passionately in love with the Buddha that he wanted to do everything for him. So one day the king said, "You wander all the time, without a home; why don't you rest during the rainy season? I'll give you my Bamboo Grove."

The spot was perfectly chosen, because the king knew that the Buddha needed a place that was pleasant and secluded but still not too far from the town so that everyone could come to hear him. Unless it was offered by a sincere disciple, the Buddha would not easily accept any gift, but he understood that Bimbisara wanted to lead the spiritual life. So he accepted the Bamboo Grove, the first gift given to the Buddha and his order, and the king gained great merit.

When we give freely, as Bimbisara did, we lighten our backlog of karma. We feel light-footed, with renewed energy for the journey. Suddenly we feel that a big lump of our burden has fallen from our shoulders.

> *Some are born again. Those caught in evil*
> *ways go to a state of intense suffering; those*
> *who have done good go to a state of joy. But*
> *the pure in heart enter nirvana.* [126]

IN THE MERCIFUL language of Hinduism and Buddhism, those who neglect the welfare of others for their own conve-

niences and comforts are not wicked; they are simply not particularly evolved. From this perspective, someone who is inor-
dinately fond of money or material possessions or food or drugs
has just come from the jungle to the city. In his previous life he
has been roaming about in the jungle with a giraffe family, trying to get leaves from the highest branches, or swimming with
fellow crocodiles in the river. Now he finds himself walking on
two legs – often with a backache, which scientists say is one
price we pay for this jump from four feet to two – and everything he sees is new.

Years ago, when I was in Minneapolis at the University of
Minnesota, one of my colleagues was worried about the Indian
students who had just come to the U.S. They would spend the
whole day in the movie theater, staying until midnight watching
every cartoon, advertisement, and preview, and then watching
the whole thing all over again.

I had to explain that in India, at least in those days, it wasn't
easy to see a movie. You usually have to stand in a long queue to
get into the theater, though there were enterprising boys who
would enter the queue early and then sell you their place. And at
the end of the movie, everyone has to leave. The management
comes and looks everywhere to make sure nobody is allowed to
stay on.

So when my colleague, rather upset, asked me what I thought
could be done to keep these students from spending all of Satur-
day at the movies, I said, "Just give them a little time."

In a month, when the novelty of seeing three or four films
over and over again had worn off, the new students from India
became just like American students – walking in and then walking out, sometimes during the first movie.

It's the same with evolution. When you have seen money – dollars, rubles, liras, rupees – over and over again, what is so special about it? When you have seen cars and trucks and trains and planes, what is so special about them? Those who are always ready to be impressed are just new – new to the school. They don't know the school motto, the school ways. But all they need is a little experience; then they too will join in singing the old school song, "One for all and all for one! Rah! Rah! Rah!"

WHEN I WAS leaving for college, my grandmother gave me sound advice. "Don't be afraid to make mistakes," she said. Nobody else told me that. All my uncles advised me to be a good boy, but because they hadn't always been good boys themselves, their advice had little effect on me. My mother, who was more compassionate, said, "Try to be a good boy." I said, "Yes, Mom, I'll try."

But my granny said: "You are going to make mistakes. Don't be afraid to fail, but when you have made a blunder, don't make excuses. Say 'I have done that. I will not do it again.'"

To err is human, but we can learn from our mistakes. Some people are so afraid of a misstep that they become paralyzed; they can't make any decision at all. It may be an important thing, it may be a small thing, but such a person cannot decide. "Shall I wear my black dress or my blue dress?" She will take out the blue dress and put it back, then take out the black dress, then the blue again. She'll keep on changing, spending precious time. Everywhere, for the indecisive person, the question is, What shall I do? What shall I do? It is much better to make a wrong decision than to make no decision at all. When you make a wrong decision and try to achieve something, you are growing. It is much better to make a wrong choice, face the consequences and learn, and then next time make the right decision.

After I went to college, when I would commit a mistake, I had the confidence to go to my grandmother and tell her what I had done. I knew she would support me, but I also knew she would take me to task. She had only to ask me one question, "How could a bright boy like you do this?" That gave me the incentive not to repeat those mistakes.

It used to hurt me frightfully, because I loved her with all my heart and could not tolerate the thought of incurring her displeasure. I would correct myself immediately because of that. If it was a friend who had led me into trouble, I would tell him, "Whatever you say, I am not coming out with you. Whatever you tempt me with, I am not going to do it." And I would stick to my bargain.

When she was convinced that I had corrected myself, Granny would come to me and say, "Come on, son, come sit by my side." Without saying a word she was telling me even if I had to suffer some sorrow, her love for me was so vast that she would rather I suffer and solve the problem so I would not have to suffer the karma of that mistake again.

If the mistake was serious, my grandmother would warn me with a question that has helped me very much, "Do you want to go through all this again?" That one question would bring me to my senses. Did I want the regret, the heartbreak, the repentance that comes to all sensitive people? If we can remember that we will have to go through all this again, it will be a stalwart protection when we are about to yield to temptation.

Granny knew how to tease me too. She would say, "How could you do all these foolish things when you know how to talk like an Englishman?" She wanted to remind me that even though I was clever enough to speak English, I wasn't clever enough never to make mistakes. That was her way of teasing me.

IN OUR LATER years we should never ask, "Why did I commit this mistake?" The right question is, "Have I learned from this mistake?" It is the splendid capacity of the human being to learn from mistakes, and therefore the second half of life can be even more beautiful than the first. During the first half of life we learn how to live. We make many mistakes, just as I have done, but in the second half of life we have wisdom and can travel towards nirvana swiftly.

When it comes to learning from mistakes, there are different degrees of capacity. There are fast learners, slow learners, and no learners. The best type, of course, is the fast learners: just one or two mistakes and they learn. They will meet with the minimum of suffering in life. Even among the saints and sages we find some who have committed grievous mistakes, but who learned quickly not to make those mistakes again.

On the other hand, ordinary people – perhaps the majority – have a medium capacity to learn and change. They need some hard knocks, which life is not slow to give. They too will learn, but later than the fast learners. Perhaps they will learn only after making many mistakes, but the important thing is they will learn.

It's the third type who get hit over and over again. They cry, get depressed, throw up their hands in despair, but do not learn. My teacher, who was unflinchingly tough, used to say, "Don't blame life. Don't blame others." Everyone has a learning capacity, she would say. If you can learn to be self-willed, she would add, you can learn not to be self-willed.

According to the Buddha, the ability to remember past failure is a precious capacity. If we were to lose that capacity, we would keep on committing mistakes, and no amount of suffering would teach us not to fall short again. It's a grim reminder from a compassionate teacher: when all discrimination is lost we will go on suffering without learning, and our precious human life is wasted. For that reason, some Buddhist texts, including the Dhammapada, remind us forcefully of the painful consequences of all the blunders we have made. These teachings must be approached with detachment, however, because without detachment dwelling on the past can become a distraction on the spiritual path.

In most cases it does not help to dwell on the past. Whatever mistakes have been committed have been committed, and let's hope we have learned our lesson. The tendency to dwell on the past and develop a guilt complex is one of the cleverest tricks of the ego. Guilt is ice cream for the ego; it can really enjoy it!

Recently, someone was telling me that he had committed terrible sins. He was shedding crocodile tears, saying, "My past has been dismal. I have committed so many mistakes."

I said, "Give me an example."

He confided in me in a conspiratorial whisper, expecting my ears to shrivel on hearing the atrocious things he had done.

After listening quietly, I said, "That doesn't sound so horrible to me."

"What?" he said. "You mean I haven't sinned?" He was out-raged.

Sometimes, even in lamenting that we have covered a whole field with wild oats, there is an attempt to boast. The ego blows up our mistakes all out of proportion so we can dwell on ourselves and how bad we are. If you want to use the term sinners, which doesn't come naturally to me, we are all small-time sinners. Instead of dwelling on how bad we are, it is much better simply to resolve not to commit those mistakes.

> *Those who are selfish suffer here and hereafter;*
> *they suffer in both worlds from the results of*
> *their own actions.*
>
> *But those who are selfless rejoice here and*
> *rejoice hereafter. They rejoice in both worlds*
> *from the results of their own actions.* (15–16)

KARMA IS NOT something imposed from outside. Everything comes from within. The law of karma states that my life is in my hands. It is I who must reap the rewards of my thoughts, words, and deeds, and it is I who must gain my own respect. No one else.

It is a matter of fact, the Buddha would say, that anyone who leads a selfish life has to reap insecurity and loneliness, followed inevitably by a lack of self-respect. The most difficult person to win over is yourself. Even if everyone else respects and admires you, you may not have self-respect. You may please everyone by putting up a front, pretending to be what you are not, but the person inside is not taken in.

In other words, I myself am judge and jury, prosecutor and

defense. The prosecutor, who is a part of me, presents the evidence, and the jury, which is also a part of me, rules guilty or not guilty. When we start forgiving others and forgetting ourselves, the defense says, "Yes, in the past he has been remiss in his behavior, but now he is learning to forgive and forbear."

"All right," the judge says, "he's a good fellow. We'll just give him a warning this time."

Sometimes, of course, the language of karma can be more extreme, to dramatize our situation. Without a certain amount of effective drama we are not likely to get the point. But there is also a humorous side to the daily sessions of the court of karma. In India we have something called the court of small causes – what Americans call small claims court. No one wants to have an elaborate trial and waste the taxpayers' money, so judgment is given on the spot. A lot of cases are brought to this court because they are small matters. You have lent your neighbor fifty dollars and he won't pay you back, so you tell him, "I'll see you in court."

Some karma is like that. Take food, for example. If you have eaten a rich pastry, the small claims court is going to be in session. The judge is going to ask, "Did you eat it?"

"Yes, your honor," you reply. "I enjoyed it very much."

The judge says, "One pound."

"Is there no alternative, your honor?"

"Yes," the judge replies. "One pound or one inch around the waist."

This is the practical language of the Buddha. Every time we are tempted to overeat or to eat the wrong foods, he reminds us that the small claims court of karma is in session.

It is an essential aspect of karma that it can only operate when the will operates. Will, according to the Buddha, is an aspect of the fourth skandha – samskara. For karma formation to take place, this skandha must come into play. In the skandhas of sensation and perception, the will does not operate, so karma cannot operate.

For example, when we say we like something or dislike something, the Buddha would say we have exercised our will because we have made a choice. If I say, "I like this, so I am going to burst into song" or "I don't like this, so I am going to start howling," I have taken on a certain karmic responsibility because I have made a choice about how to respond.

An immature person is likely not to understand that he has a choice. He will not see that he can choose to like or dislike; he will think it a matter of necessity. "I don't like this job," he will say, "therefore I am not going to do it." But according to the Buddha he can also choose to say, "I will do this job because it is important, even if I dislike it." The more heroic can add, "And I am going to enjoy it too." In making this choice he has entered into a karmic transaction, but one that leads to freedom.

The Buddha says each of us has a duty to cultivate our will. We have a duty to cultivate discrimination and learn to make right choices. We cannot refuse to choose. Therefore we live in an awfully dangerous world, because wherever the question of choice comes in, karma comes in too.

ANOTHER WAY TO understand karma is to examine the close connection between our internal state and our external environment – a connection that can be verified every day if our eyes are open.

We all know people who are accident-prone. If they bend down to pick up the Sunday paper, they fall down the steps. Wherever they go the floor is slippery or the carpet catches the heel of their shoe. Something just has to happen to make them fall. There are also people who are anger-prone. They have to be angry, because that is the mental habit they have cultivated over a long period. In today's way of life we can meet such anger-prone people every day – and sometimes they are us.

The law of karma states that wherever angry people go, they will find opportunities for anger. They will find people whom they dislike; they will encounter incidents that they don't like. If they move to a new neighborhood, the man next door will be short-tempered and the mail carrier will be irascible. If they go to the supermarket and get in the express lane, the person in front will have twenty items even though the sign says clearly there is a ten-item limit.

Simply changing the external environment will not improve the situation because that little bundle of karma will still be lodged in our backpack. We may believe that by leaving San Francisco for a small town in the mountains we will improve our chances for peace of mind. But in the mountains we will find an equal number of irascible people because that is our internal state. By moving to a new town, even a new country, we are not going to get rid of our problem.

Only a change in the internal state can enable us to function freely wherever we are – even in the midst of difficult people, even in the face of provocation. When the mind is at peace, that peace will be reflected in our outward world. When we drop in at the local bookstore, there is likely to be a friendly clerk to help us find the book we are looking for. When we go across to the café, there will be someone to serve our coffee with a smile. This is not something exceptional, because there is a connection between our state of mind and our environment.

When the Buddha uses terms such as "heaven" and "hell" he is referring to states of mind we can experience right here in this life. Violence and anger in the mind bring about a state of insecurity and despair which can truly be called hell. What is hell but estrangement from others and estrangement from oneself?

Every now and then the Buddha explains how we can be our own worst enemy in life. It is good to remind ourselves that the Buddha is telling us this out of compassion, not in an effort to pass judgment or assign blame. Selfishness is our greatest enemy, the Buddha says. Anger is its own worst enemy, and violence is the mortal foe of the violent person. As long as there is violence in our hearts, the doors to heaven will be bolted and barred against us. As long as there is rage in our hearts, we will not be allowed even to approach the gates of nirvana. Yet there have been great transformations in the Buddhist tradition that show how the most violent people have become the greatest saints.

KARMA CAN BE divided into three broad categories. First, and simplest, is "cash karma": John hits Jack, and Jack immediately hits him back.

In the second kind of karma, John has done something in the past and it is bearing fruit today. Whatever is taking place now in my life I have to face calmly, courageously, and compassionately. No amount of crying, no amount of regret, is going to undo the past. Sometimes, when we have made a mistake, we cannot help dwelling on it. Then we make a nice frame, hang the mistake on the wall, and gaze at it fondly. "Oh, how could I have made that mistake?" we say over and over again. No one benefits from this at all.

Sometimes I read curious items in the newspaper – about, say, someone who stole a small item from the corner drugstore when he was ten years old. Now he is sixty, and he writes, "Dear Abby, I have been tormented by the thought of the pen I stole when I was ten years old. Should I return the pen?"

I'm not sure what Abby would recommend, but unless the pen was gold-plated my advice would be, "Just forget it." There are occasions in life when it is necessary to make amends to someone we once offended or injured, but in order to get a particular item of karma out of our kit, it is not always necessary – or even possible – to repay the debt to a particular person. What we can do is offer help to someone else who is in need, and in that way repay the debt. That is what the Buddha means by balancing the books of karma.

Because all of us are human, all of us are likely to commit mistakes. It is essential that we be patient with ourselves – and, for the same reason, be patient with others too. The Buddha's point is, we have done it. The karma has been accumulated. The karma books have made a record of it, whether debit or credit. Once we open our eyes and become sensitive to this, life could become intolerable if we do not have compassion for ourselves. We should always remember – whatever our faults, whatever mistakes we have committed – that we can all cross the river of life by balancing the ledger of past mistakes.

When it comes to facing the karma we are reaping today, it is only natural to want to run away. In my early days I had a genius for this, but I began to notice that every time I ran away from a distressing situation, a more difficult, more painful situation would come up. At last, through my granny's guidance, the day dawned when I asked myself, Why not stay put and try to face it? I wasn't very courageous, and I certainly wasn't very calm, but I did not run away. Then I learned that once I faced my present karma, no matter what the circumstances, that karma was paid for; it would not occur again.

To be fair, this ability to face difficult situations doesn't come like a bolt from the blue. You don't wake up one fine morning and shout, "Where is this problem? I am going to stand firm and get out of this situation!" Instead most of us go slowly, supporting ourselves by leaning against any convenient wall or doorway as we learn gradually to face the predicament squarely. Most of us have to do this over and over and over again before we can extricate ourselves.

The third kind of karma is what we have sown in the past that we haven't started to harvest yet. The field is almost ripe, there is going to be a bumper crop, but the time hasn't come. This third kind of karma may be reaped next week or in the years to come – or even, the Buddha would say, in the next life.

Much better is the immediate hit of cash karma: you get in a fight and hit someone, and before you can leave, somebody else has hit you. There is a huge advantage to this because it's done with. You won't go home wondering, "When is somebody going to hit me?" You don't have to be on the defensive all the time.

With delayed karma, however, years may have passed. You've moved far away; you have changed jobs; you have a different car and a different hairstyle; and you have forgotten that old incident completely. Then you walk into a restaurant, and there is the law of karma seated in the person of your dinner guest, who attacks you in the same way you had attacked someone in the past. Once you see the connection, you know that karma can be delayed but never evaded.

On the positive side, delayed karma has one advantage: it can be reduced to a great extent. The Buddha, always practical, says that although there is nothing we can do about the karma we are reaping today, there is a good deal we can do to influence the harvest that is to come. The way to change this harvest of suffering is to go on doing good, adding to the joy of others. If you see anyone in distress, do what you can to help him. If you find people who are hungry, you can feed them; if you find people who are sick, you can help care for them. Keep forgetting yourself in the service of others, and when the time for the harvest comes, you'll find that much of the bitterness has turned to sweetness.

The liability of karma can be trimmed to an encouraging degree. First, there can be extenuating circumstances. Young people, for example, have an extra margin for making mistakes. When they do something harmful – usually out of ignorance, without understanding the consequences – their suffering may not be too severe. When young people have done damage to others or themselves without any idea how much suffering they were causing, I have often seen that as they get older they have been able to learn, to change, and have not done these thoughtless things again.

Experience is a great teacher. The American inventor Thomas Edison was once asked, "How is your work going?" Oh, splendid, he replied: "I've found seven hundred ways that don't work."

In our earlier days, most of us found seven hundred ways that didn't work. So if anyone asks you about your student days in Berkeley, you can say that you conducted an especially successful experiment on Telegraph Avenue. Don't look back upon those days with remorse and regret, because you have learned, and now you know how to compensate for the unfavorable karma reaped unwittingly in those days.

Even when we are older, if we have done something we later regret, if we work hard at making our subsequent actions more selfless, that karma will not develop fully. My granny used a grisly example to explain this. If you have blinded another's eye, she would say, the karmic result would normally be that eventually you would lose your own eye. Doesn't the Bible say "an eye for an eye"? But my grandmother would say that if you begin to help people instead of harming them, comfort people instead of hurting them, you will still receive a blow, but you will not lose your eye; perhaps you only get a bump on your forehead. It may be painful, but your karmic results are highly diminished – because the lesson has been learned.

If we can keep on making entries on the credit side, when the time of reckoning comes the credit side has been filled up. None of us need be afraid of the past if we keep on making more and more entries on the credit side.

> *As your family and friends receive you with joy*
> *when you return from a long journey, so will*
> *your good deeds receive you when you go from*
> *this life to the next, where they will be waiting*
> *for you with joy like your kinsmen.* [219–220]

WHEN COLLEGE STUDENTS in India come home for the summer vacation, there is an air of jubilation in the village.

There always seems to be someone at the bus station to recognize them, and soon the news spreads through the whole community. In my own village, the bus stop was about a mile from my home. Every summer vacation I would get down from the bus, little suitcase in hand, and before I would reach my home I would meet with a warm welcome. People would come out to ask how long I would be staying and say how glad they were to have me back.

Relationships in village India are exceptionally close. Even years later, if you meet someone you went to school with or grew up with in the village, you have to stop and talk.

Here the Buddha recalls these village scenes, but he says the only relatives that will always stand by you are your own good deeds: what is good in yourself, what is selfless in yourself. This is your real family; these are your real friends. Cultivate them always, and they will stand by you always. Your good deeds are like faithful partners who will accompany you from this life to the next, never leaving your side until you reach nirvana. Like good friends, they cheer you when you are discouraged and lighten your burden when the going gets tough.

Preparing for the inevitable journey into our next existence, the Buddha will say, is the most relevant issue in life. Making money, for example, is not good or bad; it is irrelevant. As you say in this country, you can't take it with you. If you could take it with you, it might make sense to hoard as much as you can. Similarly, if you could hoard up pleasures and put them in a safe deposit box which you could open in the hereafter, the Buddha would say, "Sure, devote your life to pleasure." But unfortunately, none of this is going to cross the border with us. In fact, very little of it gets to the border at all. We can't even carry pleasure over to the next day.

Imagine packing your gear, hoarding things, planning what you'll carry with you and what you'll send ahead. "Man," the Buddha would say, "you can't take any of this! Work on what you can take with you" – in fact, on what you can't help taking with you. Every thought we are going to take with us, every word, every deed, every desire. Those which do not bear fruit in this life will bear fruit in the next, as they go on shaping our destiny.

There is no such thing as a little thought, no such thing as an unimportant act. Therefore, the Buddha says, we should not blame others for our lot. We always have a choice in what we think, and as we think, so we live.

> *The compulsive urges of the thoughtless grow*
> *like a creeper. They jump like a monkey from*
> *one life to another, looking for fruit in the*
> *forest.* [334]

> *As a tree, though cut down, recovers and*
> *grows if its roots are not destroyed, suffering*
> *will come to you more and more if these*
> *compulsive urges are not extinguished.* [338]

THE ROOT OF karma, and hence of suffering, is the selfish desires and selfish cravings that parch the throat while we believe they are quenching our thirst. The key word here is selfish. The Buddha points out that there are right desires, which contribute to our own happiness and to the happiness of those around us, but there are also wrong desires, which contribute not only to our sorrow but at the same time to the sorrow of those around us. When right desires come – to contribute to the happiness of others, to contribute to the peace of the world – we should yield to them with joy, act on them with enthusiasm. But many personal desires are wrong desires, compulsive urges, which will bring us only suffering.

In my early days I too had many desires, most of them comparatively harmless. Once I took to meditation, however, I came to see that they were holding me back. Even so, it wasn't easy for me to withdraw myself from them and pull my attention away.

Once, someone sincerely dedicated to deepening his meditation came to me and admitted candidly, "I find this so painful!" I wanted to rejoin, "Don't be under the impression that I found it jolly good fun." I found it painful too, but more and more I wanted to cross the river at last, so I began to free myself from personal desires. And gradually, instead of finding it painful, I began to find it gratifying.

In the old days, before meditation, my initial response to an opportunity for personal pleasure or ambition was to go after it – and not only go after it, but go after it with a vengeance. Today, my initial response to any selfish desire is to resist it. Today, this has become a natural response. If it is an unwelcome desire, I have only to tell it no. If it is a more innocent desire, I am free to say, "Let's yield within reason." Naturally, our first response to a selfish desire is to run after it, but our response should be just the opposite: to sit back and examine the desire carefully.

When a desire comes down the runway, you say, "Yes, you look very nice in your Paris gown and your Spanish shoes. Now turn round." And at the back there is a big tear. The front is all right, but the back is a rag. When you're able to view your desires with detachment, often they don't look very nice. When you look at the long-term consequences, they don't look inviting. We run after desires because they look nice, but when we are able to judge, we say, "If this improves my health and security, I will yield to it. If it does not, I will not yield."

We should never feel discouraged if we have strong desires, because desires can be transformed. People with a lot of selfish desires will have a lot of selfless power if they can transform those desires. People who have a lot of physical passion, if they can transfer it into spiritual passion, will go far on the spiritual path. This is the paradox: sometimes those who are boiling with passion can go much farther than those who lack desire.

Desire is power. The deeper our desire, the greater our power. This is difficult to grasp. It may even seem a contradiction. But we can understand it if we see that, like electricity, desire is a flowing source of energy. People who have huge desires, which means a lot of drive, can go a long, long way on the Buddha's path. But like electricity, if we are to use desire for the spiritual journey, it must be under our control. And it must be increasingly selfless. Otherwise our burden of karma will increase, making progress on the spiritual path harder and harder.

When those who are foolish become wise,
they give light to the world like the full moon
breaking through the clouds.

When their good deeds overcome the bad, they
give light to the world like the moon breaking
free from behind the clouds. [172–173]

SOMETIMES A SIMPLE story can strike a healthy blow, forcing us to change while our head is still making up excuses. Such a story is the account of the meeting of the Buddha with a heartless robber bearing the grim name of Angulimala, "he who wears a garland made of fingers" – the fingers of those he has killed. The whole world was afraid of Angulimala; no one wanted to come near him. But not the Buddha. One day the Blessed One was walking along a lonely path in the forest where Angulimala operated, and the robber, used to seeing people shun him, was startled to see a splendid figure in a saffron robe walking along, radiating peace and love.

With sword in hand, Angulimala cried out, "Stop!"

With a serene smile, the Buddha walked on.

The robber had never met anyone who was not afraid of him. "Didn't you hear what I said?" he cried. "Stop!"

"I have stopped," the Buddha replied, "but you have not."

Beginning to feel the infinite compassion of the Buddha, the robber asked him, "What do you mean?"

"I have stopped injuring others," the Buddha replied, "but you have not."

Angulimala stood speechless.

The Buddha continued, "Do you want to undertake a battle

that requires a courage that will not flinch and a valor that will not flag?"

Angulimala said, "Yes, show me the foe!"

The Buddha replied, "He is in your heart."

The robber bowed before the Buddha and said, "Teach me how to fight this battle."

The Buddha taught Angulimala that hatred shuts the door on the kingdom of nirvana, while those who are prepared to undertake the heroic battle of extinguishing anger and greed can achieve nirvana in this very life.

Blessed by the Buddha, Angulimala became the gentlest of monks. He did not look back, but devoted himself selflessly to the welfare of all. Yet many years later, while begging for alms in Savatthi, the villagers attacked him with rocks and sticks, for though he wore the saffron robe of a monk they could not forget his past cruelty. Angulimala was struck on his body and his head, and blood flowed down from his wounds. Yet he did not fight back, and forgave his attackers because he understood that in this way he could undo the karma of his former crimes and suffer no more in the next life. He bore all this suffering patiently with perfect love.

> As a cowherd with his staff drives cows to fresh
> fields, old age and death lead all creatures to
> new lives. [135]

IN OUR INDIAN villages, the cowherd is an important man. In the beautiful village in Kerala where I grew up, our cowherd, Apu, was a popular figure known to everyone. Every morning at sunrise Apu would come to each house in the village, and as soon as he reached the gate, someone from each family would untie their cows and give them to Apu to take to the meadow to graze.

Here the Buddha gives us the tender image of death as a cowherd, driving us on to the next life, where we take on a new body. We come again as a little Tommy or a little Rebecca. Is this not a matter for congratulation? We get so happy when we have a new car. Having a new body is much the same. The profundity of it and the promise of it takes away the fear of death.

When death comes, the Buddha teaches, it is not the closing of a door; it is an opening. It is not the end of a story but the beginning of another chapter. Not only is this life in our hands but even the life to come. This is the deep significance of the concept of karma.

TO TRULY BEGIN to reduce the load of karma, we must understand what the Buddha means by "mind," which will be the topic of our next chapter. Perhaps the most significant teaching in the entire Dhammapada concerns this link between mind, karma, and destiny.

> *Our life is shaped by our mind; we become*
> *what we think. Suffering follows an evil*
> *thought as the wheels of a cart follow the oxen*
> *that draw it.*

Our life is shaped by our mind; we become what we think. Joy follows a pure thought like a shadow that never leaves. [1–2]

◇ *The Inner Journey*

IN SPITE OF its triumphs, modern civilization pays little attention to the vital skill of training the mind, which is the foundation of the spiritual life. Where the body is concerned we take training for granted, but we believe that the mind cannot be trained. We have forgotten the wisdom of the sages of India who discovered that just as the body can be trained, there is nothing miraculous about training the mind. The same enthusiasm, the same discipline, the same dedication that goes into becoming a ballet dancer or an Olympic champion can allow the mind to perform what to us seem miracles.

> *Mules are good animals when trained; even better are well-trained Sind horses and great elephants. Best among men is one with a well-trained mind.* [322]

> *Be like a well-trained horse, swift and spirited, and go beyond sorrow through faith, meditation, and energetic practice of the dharma.* [144]

EVEN IF WE accept that the mind can be trained, it's not going to be easy, primarily for three reasons. First, the mind is turbulent – to be blunt, often quarrelsome, ill-mannered, and contrary. Rather than riding on a swift steed to nirvana, to use the Buddha's image, we find we have a monkey mind as a companion on our journey.

A famous Sanskrit verse says this is a monkey that is drunk, stung by a scorpion, and possessed by a ghost – all at the same time. The next time you go to the zoo, just watch a monkey jumping from branch to branch. Now imagine it is drunk and has been stung by a scorpion. I don't know how many of you have seen a scorpion, but I hope nobody has been stung; it's a terrible experience. And on top of all this, this already restive creature has been possessed by a ghost.

Naturally this monkey causes us a lot of trouble. The restless mind is thinking all the time, running on constantly without any conscious control. A mind that is in frantic motion all the time will leap from activity to activity, much of it unnecessary and even harmful. Often problems arise simply because all this inner bustle – the endless chaos of thoughts, memories, impulses, and desires – consumes a lot of energy.

Second, the mind is a very, very clever customer that doesn't really want to be our friend. When we begin to take steps to train it, we are met with turmoil and rebellion, sometimes expressed so subtly that we really have to hand it to the mind for being so cunning.

The third reason the mind is so hard to train is its power and speed. With a little reflection it is easy to see that the mind usually wanders about virtually free of any restraint. In short, the mind "goes where it likes and does what it wants." It travels far and wide without physical restrictions, and it needs no special time and place to travel.

When summer arrives many people want to travel, but they can't simply hop on a plane and go to Germany or India or Iceland. The authorities will say, "Where is your passport?" But the mind travels like a powerful potentate who needs neither passport nor visa and never has to pass through security. It can go anywhere it wants anytime. If I think of India now, in the blink of an eye I am in Kerala. That's what the mind is able to do. No advance in technology, however amazing, will ever bring about a vehicle as fast as the mind, which is much faster than the speed of light. That is the power of the mind, which the Buddha says we have to train. That is why it is so tremendously difficult. If the mind could manage to cross the street only with great effort, it would be easy to train – but then the rewards of training would be inconsequential too.

> As an archer aims an arrow, the wise aim their
> restless thoughts, hard to aim, hard to restrain.
> [33]

IF WE WANT to train the mind, if we want to aim our thoughts as an archer aims an arrow, the practice of meditation is the way to achieve it. Because it is the basic tool for training the mind, meditation is always at the very heart of Buddhist practice.

Somerset Maugham, the British author of *The Razor's Edge*, was tormented by life's deeper questions and while traveling in India he went out of his way to meet spiritual seekers and teachers. Finally, he asked one teacher how the power of meditation could be acquired. After listening carefully to the instructions, he took the plunge.

"That evening," Maugham wrote, "I did as he had directed. I took the time before I began. I remained in that state for so long that I thought I must have by far exceeded the quarter of an hour he had prescribed. I looked at my watch. Three minutes had passed. It had seemed an eternity."

For nearly all of us, a first try at meditation brings a revelation very much like this. Abruptly, it dawns on us that it is a euphemism to say we think our thoughts. Actually our thoughts think us. They are in command, and we unwittingly serve them. Therefore, when we try to direct our thoughts at will during meditation, or even while focusing on a task, we find that the mind – this ever-shifting bundle of thoughts, memories, desires, fears, urges, anxieties, and aspirations – has a mind of its own.

When Maugham first tried to meditate, this brilliant novelist must have thought, "This is something that I can easily learn. I have written plays. I have written novels. I can do anything with my mind. Why can't I learn to meditate?" Only when he closed his eyes and tried to keep his mind still did he discover how impossible the task is.

Just like Maugham, we too are likely to sit down to meditate for the first time with great confidence, only to have a rude awakening. Yet there are a few rare individuals whose experience is quite different. These are the great saints and sages in all religions. While in India, Maugham sought out one such man, Ramana Maharshi, one of our great sages in South India, who had stilled his mind completely at a very young age. Profoundly moved by the experience of meeting this remarkable sage, Maugham later based the saint in *The Razor's Edge* on him.

Such figures are extremely rare. In the Hindu and Buddhist scriptures it is said that such rapid illumination can come only as the fruit of much effort in previous lives. In the case of most of us, myself included, it requires many years of difficult discipline to begin to master the mind. Even the Buddha had to struggle for years – according to tradition, for many lives. So none of us need be disheartened if we find this an uphill climb, a difficult ascent that at times seems almost impossible.

> *What use is matted hair? What use is a*
> *deerskin on which to sit for meditation if*
> *your mind still seethes with lust? Saffron robe*
> *and outward show do not make a brahmin,*
> *but training of the mind and senses through*
> *practice of meditation.* [394–395]

LIKE A TRUE but demanding teacher, the Buddha says that all the external disciplines we see practiced in many parts of the world will not help us cross the river of life. We don't require external aids to attain what is essentially an internal experience.

In India you will often see people with certain marks on their forehead or a necklace of holy beads as outward signs of a spiritual quest. Members of the monastic order wear saffron-colored robes. But there are also others who do not practice any disciplines who wear these things to give the impression that they too are practicing disciplines. The Buddha is reminding us that these outward displays have nothing to do with training the mind.

This applies to fasting too. We want to keep the body strong, and fasting is not going to do that. We don't have to be embarrassed about eating nourishing food and wearing nice clothes; that will not take away from our spiritual awareness – and no amount of outward show will add to our spiritual awareness if the mind is in turmoil and uncontrolled.

> *Hard it is to train the mind, which goes where it likes and does what it wants. But a trained mind brings health and happiness. The wise can direct their thoughts, subtle and elusive, wherever they choose: a trained mind brings health and happiness.* [35–36]

MOST OF US will try anything else first, even fasting, before we will challenge the mind. That is why the Buddha reminds us that no amount of physical effort is going to bring the mind under control. No amount of physical effort is going to bring enlightenment if the mind is not trained.

The Buddhist scriptures tell of many of young Siddhartha's experiences in his search for truth, and some of these stories are meant to be appalling, to warn us that not even these tremendous physical exploits enabled him to attain his goal. After the Buddha took leave of his charioteer Channa, he wandered for years in the forests visiting sages, philosophers, and yogis, always asking for the way beyond death. Some of these teachers put great emphasis on physical disciplines such as fasting and breathing exercises.

The young prince, though he grew up in a palace surrounded by luxury, threw himself without reservation into this harsh way of life. When his first teacher told him that by holding the breath for a certain number of counts and then breathing out, he would be able to train the mind, the Buddha-to-be responded with tremendous enthusiasm. "Why observe this counting of breaths?" he asked himself. "Why not hold the breath until the mind is destroyed?"

This gives us an idea of the resolve of young Siddhartha. If we had met him in his early days, we would have been frightened by his immense capacity and unbreakable will to follow such disciplines in his search for enlightenment. He warns us not to try to emulate him because he soon found that his body was weakened by this painful struggle, and his mind was disturbed and even more unruly. He left the ashram where these harsh methods were practiced, and later he would tell his disciples what he had tried and what he had learned.

After breathing exercises, his next experiments were with fasting. There are excruciating descriptions of the deprivation he endured. "After that," he says, "I thought to myself: Now suppose I practice utter abstinence from food. Suppose I feed myself on just a little food, a mere morsel now and then, such as the juice of a bean." This Buddha has a strange sense of humor: take one soybean, put it in the blender, juice it, and serve the juice for dinner. Predictably, his body soon reached a state of utter exhaustion.

"Just as the rafters of a tottering house fall in this way and that," he recalled to his monks, "so did my ribs fall in this way and that, through that lack of sustenance. Just as in a deep, deep well, the sparkle of the waters may be seen sunk in the deeps below, so in the depths of their sockets did the luster of my eyes seem sunk through that same lack of sustenance. Just as a bitter gourd cut off unripened from the stalk is shriveled and withered by wind and sun, so the very skin of my head shriveled and withered through lack of food."

I can imagine his disciples collapsing when they hear all this. Surely, after this they no longer heard anything else the Buddha had to say!

The Buddha relates this to warn the monks not to compete with each other in austerity, because none of them would be able to outdo him. Nobody has ever beaten the Buddha in mortification, and nobody will be able to beat him in the future. That is why his experiments are so significant. None of this, he discovered, would help him attain nirvana. He narrates these frightful experiences to warn us that not even the most tremendous physical exploits can help us cross the river of life. We need a strong body and a resilient nervous system if we want to train the mind.

> Going about with matted hair, without food or
> bath, sleeping on the ground smeared with dust,
> or sitting motionless – no amount of penance
> can help a person whose mind is not purified.
>
> But one whose mind is serene and chaste,
> whose senses are controlled and whose life
> is nonviolent – these are true brahmins,
> true monks, even if they wear fine clothes.
> [141–142]

HAVING DISCOVERED THAT austerity was not the way to calming the mind, Siddhartha began casting about for another approach, and there came to his mind an experience he had had under a rose apple tree long before.

At the age of seven or eight, he recalled, he had gone to the annual plowing festival, where his father ceremonially guided the bullocks in plowing the first furrow. It was a long, hot day, and when the boy grew sleepy his family set him down to rest on a platform under a rose apple tree. When they returned hours later, they found him seated upright in the same position as they had left him. Disturbed by the ceaseless toil of the bullocks and plowmen and the plight of the tiny creatures who lost their homes and lives in the plowing, Siddhartha had become absorbed in reflection on the transience of life, and because of the disciplines he had undergone in previous lives he slipped naturally into a higher mode of knowing. In this profound absorption he forgot himself and his surroundings completely, and joy suffused his consciousness.

For those who want to follow in the footsteps of the Buddha it is necessary to keep the body at its best, to maintain physical health. A healthy body is a valuable aid to controlling the mind. When you have a healthy, strong body and mind, it's much easier to meditate, much easier to work hard, much easier to sleep well.

IN ORDER TO make a friend of the mind, there is an important first step: we have to realize, at least provisionally, that we are not the mind.

For those of us who have been conditioned to believe that we are the mind – which is to say virtually everyone today – it will come as a shock to read the teachings of the Buddha on this point. With the principle of the five skandhas, the Buddha says first that we are not the body, but also that we are not the mind – not the collection of sensations, perceptions, samskaras, and consciousness that make up who we think we are. To understand that we are not the body takes many years of spiritual work, but that is only the beginning; unzipping this mental identification is much harder.

I too used to think I was my mind, but after many years of work in meditation, I now look upon my body as my external instrument and my mind as my internal instrument. This is one of the most thrilling discoveries we can make in meditation, because it means that we don't have to act on our states of mind. We don't have to allow ourselves to be affected by mental states. Even if selfish thoughts, resentments, or any other kind of negative thoughts arise, we don't have to act on them; we don't have to own them. Even before we reach nirvana, this brings a wonderful peace.

As long as we believe that we are the mind, we are likely to be subject to a good deal of turmoil. Caught up in our thoughts and emotions, often in reaction to the thoughts and emotions of others, we cannot escape the tumult of the mind. We make such inaccurate statements as "I am angry, I am afraid, I am greedy." Actually it is our mind that is angry, afraid, or greedy, but this is just a passing mental state. Our real nature, which Buddhists call our Buddha-nature, knows neither anger nor fear, neither greed nor malice, neither animosity nor resentment.

When you get detached from the body, as I have been saying, you take good care of it. Similarly, when you understand that

of mind. But as the whirling movement of that torch slows down, the circle begins to flicker; we see more and more just a glowing torch. When the movement comes to a stop, we now see that the circle of fire was an illusion. Similarly, it is the speed of the mind – the speed with which thoughts chase one another – that deludes us into believing that the stream of consciousness is continuous.

Unfortunately, in most human beings there is an inherent tendency for the mind to speed up. In the case of a person who is in great torment, perhaps overcome by anger or fear, the torch is whirling so fast it is out of control. Thoughts are thinking themselves; they cannot be stopped, no matter how hard we try. We all know how in moments of great distress we think to ourselves, "If only I could stop thinking! If only my mind would quiet down." We can make a kind of equation between the speed of thought and the grade of anguish: the faster the thinking, the greater the anguish; the slower the thinking, the less the anguish. No thinking, no anguish: "This not arising, that does not arise."

If we can grasp the idea of kshanikavada, it will give us insight into how the thinking process can be changed. Let me demonstrate this with a basket of lemons. (I choose lemons because most thoughts are what people call lemons.) Take five lemons and arrange them in a line, all touching. If you push the first lemon, the last lemon will move. The Buddha tells us to just move the lemons apart. Don't keep them next to each other; put a wider and wider distance between them. Then you can touch the first lemon and the last one will say, "It doesn't bother me."

In other words, if you can see the mind as it really is, you will see that one thought doesn't touch the next. Do you see the utter simplicity of it? I have heard that some of the greatest discoveries in science are noted for their simplicity. Here is one of the greatest discoveries about the mind, so remarkable yet so simple a child can understand.

Yet although it is easy to understand this, it is very, very hard to still the mind. For that there is only one way: the regular practice of meditation.

> *There can be no meditation for those who are*
> *not wise, and no wisdom for those who do*
> *not meditate. Growing in wisdom through*
> *meditation, you will surely be close to nirvana.*
> [372]

MEDITATION ENABLES US to see into the heart of things. As concentration increases in the great journey into the depths of consciousness, we begin to see deeply into the nature of things. Over and over again the Buddha will say that meditation is the source of wisdom.

It is primarily through the practice of meditation that knowledge is brought down from the head to the heart, where it becomes wisdom. It's a long, long way from the head to the heart, and for most of us this transformation of intellectual knowledge into heart-knowledge takes many, many years.

*If you meditate earnestly, pure in mind and
kind in deeds, leading a disciplined life in
harmony with the dharma, you will grow in
glory.*

*If you meditate earnestly, through spiritual
disciplines you can make an island for yourself
that no flood can overwhelm.* [24–25]

BECAUSE IT IS so central to all spiritual practice, let me take a few moments here to review some basic principles regarding meditation.

One, meditation is a discipline. It is not letting the mind wander. Second, meditation is not divorced from life; it yields rich dividends: on the physical level, the emotional level, the intellectual level, and of course on the spiritual level. You don't have to leave home to learn to meditate; you can be married or you can be single; you can hold any job that is not at the expense of life. You can wear a three-piece suit or well-worn jeans. There is no need to shave your head or grow a beard. None of this has anything to do with the spiritual life and meditation.

Third, it is good to remember that all of us begin meditation against heavy odds. We have allowed our mind to run wild for a long, long time, so we shouldn't get impatient to discover that we cannot keep the mind under control even for a few moments.

Training the mind through meditation cannot be achieved quickly or through violent means. Complete sovereignty over the mind can be achieved only little by little, day by day, step by step. Don't get impatient, and don't get angry with the mind. That is just what the mind wants! Infinite patience and intelligent practice are required for steady progress. Right from the early days, therefore, on the one hand, we should be patient – and not only in the early days, but for years and years. And on the other hand, we should always be persistent and vigilant. We need to keep on trying with a kind of patient impatience, which is quite a difficult skill to learn.

My advice for those who are beginning the practice of meditation is always to respect the mind. Respect your mind and the mind will respect you. Don't think that the mind is slow-witted. I assure you, the mind is a clever customer with quite a few cards up its sleeve. Unless you are prepared to use artistry and skill, the clever mind will win the hand time after time. Always treat the mind as a friend, not an adversary, and eventually it will come to have such respect for you that it no longer tries to play tricks on you.

In meditation, the mind has to be coaxed and cajoled. Sometimes it must be rewarded and at other times gently reasoned with. The mind is very much like a little child – not wicked but willful, always ready to say no. I've always found it astonishing how early children start saying no. Even a little fellow hardly out of his cradle is screaming *no, no, no, no* at the top of his lungs. The mind is just like that. When you are angry and try to coax your mind, "Don't be angry, be sympathetic," the mind will just cry, "No, no, no, no!" When you're afraid, try telling your mind not to be afraid. The mind says, "Waaa! I cannot help being afraid!" – which is another way of saying no.

My suggestion is to meditate at the same time every morning. To meditate one day at six-thirty, another day at seven-thirty, and the next day at eight-thirty will get you nowhere. You may say you have met the requirement, and that is true; you have. But the mind is laughing at you. There is no regularity, there is no discipline, which is just what the mind appreciates. If you can keep a fixed period for meditation, the mind will gradually learn that at that time at least it will have a temporary abdication. It is quite sure that it is going to have a re-coronation soon, but at least for that meditation period you can pretend that you are master in your own home, and that the mind is a transient who has moved in against your better judgment.

Gradually you will find that you don't need an alarm clock to wake up at the right time for meditation. You will get up at the same time because that has become a habit, just as it will become a habit for your mind to quiet down at that time. And you will enjoy getting up early because that is the best time for meditation: as night turns to day, the mind quiets down naturally.

Most spiritual teachers tell us that it is a great help if we can meditate together with a few others. If you are a bit late, there is always somebody to say afterwards, "You came rather late, didn't you?" Or if you miss your meditation one morning, somebody will say, "We missed you. Where did you go? L.A.?" These awkward questions are usually motivated by a sincere concern, and when we know others care about our meditation we have a valuable reason to sustain our efforts. Even when we don't feel equal to meditation, why not just go for meditation and shield ourselves from Paul Pry?

In meditation we are actually playing with the mind, which in some ways is like handling a powerful explosive. Whenever we sink below the surface level of consciousness, potent resources are slowly being released into our lives. These resources must be used; they must be harnessed. As you meditate more deeply, you should work more – on the physical level, the intellectual level, the creative level – without thought of profit or pleasure. When the energy released in meditation is channeled into selfless service, we will proceed safely and swiftly on the spiritual path.

It is essential to have physical exercise appropriate for our state of health, and work that benefits others, what the Buddha calls Right Occupation. We need to turn outwards in work and in affectionate human relationships, because one of the serious dangers of deepening meditation is the longing to take shelter inside. Inside, everything feels so warm, while the world outside can seem so cold. Outside, people look so frigid, events look so unappealing; inside there is such warmth and shelter that you feel you could stay and sit forever by the fire. It is good to spend time with people even if they – or we – are not always agreeable; that is how we restore the mind to health.

The method of meditation I have used for many decades involves sitting quietly with eyes closed and going slowly, in the mind, through the words of an inspirational passage that appeals to me deeply. It might be a prayer, or a poem from one of the great mystics, or a piece of scripture from any of the world's religions, for example, the first chapter of the Dhamma-pada. When I sit in meditation, I go through the words of the Buddha's verses slowly, with deep concentration, letting every precious word sink deeply into my awareness. Now, after long practice, the words of the inspirational passage have permeated my consciousness. That is the test of meditation – not heavenly sounds and visions, but how we respond in daily relations at home, at work, and even on the bus with fellow passengers. I have been meditating for decades, but even now I still catch myself saying, "There is nothing like meditation!"

NOW THAT THE basics of training the mind are out of the way, let me change the metaphor and describe the mind as the terrain of the journey itself. With that change in perspective, we can see that the entire journey to nirvana is an excursion into the world of the mind.

As always, it is easier to understand this through a story. This one is about what took place when the Buddha sat under the bodhi tree and proclaimed the words that echo in the heart of every true spiritual aspirant everywhere: "Come what may, let my bones melt away, let my blood dry up, I will not get up until I have entered nirvana!"

Sitting in meditation with head, neck, and spine in a straight line, holding his body motionless and his mind at rest, he spoke these words with such absolute authority that the sutras say the bodhi tree burst into blossom and covered him with flowers. After countless lifetimes, he knew the time had come for his plunge into nirvana. But first he had to travel into the depths of consciousness and confront Mara once and for all.

That night, Mara brought all his forces to the attack – first his daughters, voluptuous forms representing pleasure, who began their seductive dance fully expecting Siddhartha to succumb to all the old blandishments, forget his spiritual destiny, and fall back into the arms of the world.

To their surprise, the Buddha was not tempted, and Mara's daughters retreated in despair. Now it was time for the mob of Mara's henchmen to attack, offering power beyond the dreams of the worst tyrant and prestige and wealth beyond all worldly aspiration. When these offers of wealth and power were refused, they did not go away quietly but turned into demonic shapes with fearful weapons to continue the attack.

The description of Mara in the Buddhist scriptures is amazingly contemporary. He tempts with sex, tempts with power, strikes through every human weakness. Today, twenty-five hundred years later, Mara still tempts in all the old ways and perhaps in a few newer ones, such as drugs and the powerful media. It is not an exaggeration to say that some of the movies today look as if they were produced and directed by Mara. Mara's cohorts are there on the screen, and his daughters make their appearance as well. Today we are still under the age-old spell of Mara because even now we are utterly identified with our physical existence. You might say that Mara is a very important person in today's world, a celebrity who travels in a long motorcade with powerful forces at his command.

But Mara can also be charming. When his armies failed to shake Siddhartha's resolve, Mara appeared in his most reasonable and urbane form. He played his first card, saying, "You don't know what is in store for you in nirvana. Don't try to cross into that unknown world. It is better to stay on this level of consciousness, where you at least know what to expect."

The Buddha sits quietly, not shaken at all. "Go on, Mara, reveal yourself, shoot your arrows. I am not afraid of you."

Mara is conquered for now – though he'll be back – and the Buddha begins his journey into the depths of consciousness.

Fortunately, the Buddha himself describes the stages of this journey, passing through what I would call the personal unconscious into the collective unconscious and plumbing its depths until he reached nirvana. Giving a rough outline, the Buddhist sutras describe the journey as taking place in stages, which can be helpful in understanding our own journey in meditation.

First, we all begin on the surface level of consciousness, which is the normal waking state. The Buddha would regard this as a rather low level of awareness because here we don't have access to any of our deeper resources. This is essentially a physical level. Mighty things can be accomplished in the physical world, and there is no reason to belittle these accomplishments, which have made life more comfortable and brought us great technological achievements. But modern civilization thinks this is the only state of consciousness, and that is where tragedy strikes because so much more of what a human being can draw on lies in the depths below.

Just below the surface of consciousness we enter the first stage of meditation, which is characterized by distractions. Even the Buddha had to pass through this stage to go deeper, so none of us need be embarrassed if we sit down to meditate and find we have distractions about the work we will be doing later in the day and the problems that are on our hands. It takes a certain amount of time to pack everything away and draw a little curtain so that these distractions can be left behind. When we come out of meditation, we can pick them all up again so that we can face the challenges of the day. This stage is essentially a clearance of luggage, putting things away, establishing some order.

Deeper in the personal unconscious, once we gain the capacity to put distractions aside, we find that countless things impede our progress. Everywhere there are red lights: likes and dislikes, sensory cravings, personal attachments. We wait for the lights to turn green . . . and wait, and wait, but they don't change. "All right," we say at first, "I'll wait. The light has to change sometime." But time passes, the light is still red, and we start to get frustrated, "Let the light turn green!" Then one day we get a yellow light. When you see the yellow light, make a dash for it! Only for people like the Buddha does the light turn green.

At these depths in the personal unconscious everything gets much more subtle. Sometimes you can't see the obstacle; you can't get hold of the impediments at all. Progress gets more sticky because the challenges are more subtle. Challenges on the surface level are obvious, because they are mostly physical. If you don't want to eat candy, for example, nobody is going to put candy into your mouth. It requires some effort to resist a temptation like this, but the temptation is clear, and everybody is capable of dealing with physical temptations. Once you dive below the surface level, however, you find a very strange world.

In changing levels of consciousness like this, one recurrent difficulty is the problem of sleep. At each new level we are like a child learning to walk. We know how to walk on the surface level of the mind, but we don't know how to walk in the dark realms of the unconscious, so the easiest thing for the mind to do is to black out. This is simply the mind saying, "I don't know how to walk here, so I'm going to fall asleep."

This image of falling is an apt one, because all kinds of vague fears come up when we are about to change levels in meditation. We can't name those fears or face them, so we just go to sleep. Again, this is just the mind saying, "I don't want to have anything to do with this!"

When you are changing from one level of consciousness to another, you find that your will has been left behind; that is why you slumber. It can be depressing: every time you sit down to meditate, you fall asleep. The brighter side is that you are no longer on the surface level. The will hasn't kept up, so you have to say to it, "Come along!"

There are two ways to tackle the problem, and both are needed. First, you can begin to look for opportunities during the day when you can strengthen the will. Second, when you find yourself getting drowsy in meditation, draw yourself away from your back support, sit up straight, and fight the wave of sleep. You'll find that simply straightening the spinal column has a beneficial effect on concentration. But even when you do everything in your power to sit up straighter and stay awake, you may not be able to; that's what lack of will means. And even if you do stay awake, after a while the wave of sleep will come over you again, and the same story will repeat itself. This can go on for a long time.

These are likely to be unwelcome suggestions, because when you are on the verge of sleep in meditation, the feeling is one of delicious relaxation. At that time the expression on your face is blissful. All is right in the world, God is in his heaven, and here I am asleep. You look so happy, so contented. "Isn't this great!" I don't like being a wet blanket, but I must tell you that in order to wake up on a deeper level of consciousness, this is the time to make a real effort of will, draw yourself up, and stick it out with all the doggedness you can muster.

Give or take a few weaknesses, our willpower may function fairly well on the level of waking life, but below the conscious level the will just doesn't operate. That is why learning to walk there is so difficult. It is by meditating regularly day in and day out, week in and week out, year in and year out, that we learn to operate in these subterranean areas.

This problem is not always what we usually call sleep. At a certain depth in meditation we are neither awake nor asleep, neither in the world within nor the world outside. This state is called "the sleep of yoga," and it descends like a blanket.

Most professionals I have talked to on this subject maintain that it is impossible to be awake in this state – to be conscious in the unconscious. Psychologists will tell you you're wasting your time. But this is precisely what we are doing in meditation: learning to wake up on a deeper level of consciousness.

If we fall asleep at this level, between a shallower state of consciousness and a deeper one, we cannot go deeper; we just stay on the surface. What we need to do at that point is take one leap and fall in. When the time comes to leap, leap; don't hold back. There is a point where we can pull back, but if we go a little further, there is a point of no return when even if we try to sleep, we won't be able to. Then we slip into a deeper level of consciousness.

There is no need to be despondent over these recurring episodes of drowsiness. This is a reassuring sign that the nervous system is relaxing. As long as we are making the effort to stay awake, there is no failure. It is when we stop making an effort and yield to the wave of sleep that our meditation actually stops. Then there is no more meditation. Instead of going deeper vertically, we are going off horizontally. All kinds of things can take place when we lose our hold on our attention. If I may sound a note of caution, there is even the possibility that we may wander into an Alice's Wonderland where the demarcation line between fact and fantasy becomes dimmer and dimmer.

Please don't be under the impression that the struggle to resist sleep is a vain effort. Every time we do this we are strengthening our will. It's only a matter of time before we find that we can overcome these waves of drowsiness and make the change to a deeper level of consciousness.

> This is the path; there is no other that leads to
> the purification of the mind. Follow this path
> and conquer Mara. This path will lead to the
> end of suffering. This is the path I made known
> after the arrows of sorrow fell away. [274–275]

IN DEEP MEDITATION, when we are far below the world of surface sensations and perceptions, we begin to perceive, dimly at first, the samskaras that lurk there, which are frightening enough. But, finally, we will face the awful power of our biggest enemy: *tanha,* the obsessive thirst for separate satisfaction. Here, the Buddha says, we finally face the real foe. Only then do we begin to see how many of our difficulties are due to Mara, our greatest enemy, who corrupts and consumes everything.

But Mara is an elusive antagonist. Many years on the spiritual path are spent just reaching the point where we can take him on. In the deeper stages of meditation we will experience some of the most challenging encounters a human being can face. At these times we shouldn't get upset or despondent because we are protected by a very delicate timing: we reach Mara's den only when we have gained the capacity to look at him with detachment, understanding, courage, and control. So we can assure ourselves that even though beasts prowl about in the depths of our consciousness, by incessant valor and unceasing discipline, we can learn to tame them.

To have all the adventure you want, you don't have to go to Africa or India. You can just take a good look deep inside, down into the collective unconscious, to watch an endless parade of the wildest, most treacherous animals that ever wandered the earth. It is because we believe that the world within is a cultivated garden that we get surprised when we come across a tiger on the trail or a leopard slinking behind a tree. Leopards, you know, don't say, "Good morning, may I eat you?" They leap at your throat. Saints and sages like the Buddha know this. They understand that in our long, long evolution we have all passed through these stages. Even if we do not accept the words of the Buddha, if we accept only Darwin's concept of evolution, we can understand that these creatures in the unconscious are the vestiges of our animal past.

In the Buddhist scriptures there are many stories, called Jatakas, about the Buddha's past lives. I think the Buddha must have entertained his disciples with these stories of his previous incarnations. In one delightful episode he describes how he was a tiger. It must have been a most exhilarating moment to hear the Compassionate One confessing that he had been a tiger. He also says that his wife, Yashodhara, the sweetest, gentlest, loveliest of women, had been a tigress. In a sense he must have been entertaining his disciples, but at the same time he was assuring all of us that these are natural stages of evolution. There is tragedy only if we get stuck in the tiger's skin. The relics of those stages are still with us, like specimens in a museum.

*One day's glimpse of the deathless state is
better than a hundred years of life without it.
One day's glimpse of dharma is better than a
hundred years of life without it.* [114–115]

THE BORDERLAND BETWEEN the personal unconscious and the collective unconscious is very, very hard even to reach, and once reached it seems as impenetrable as the Great Wall of China. Somehow, we have to breach this solid wall, and that can take a long, long time. Progress can be painfully, frustratingly slow. First, we need to learn to direct our attention like a laser in order to drill a little hole and force an entrance barely large enough to squeeze through. Then we widen the hole until we have a proper gap and can put up a little sign: "Welcome." We begin to feel confident. It still takes time to go in and come out, but we know now how to do it. We are beginning to feel at ease.

But progress comes in fits and starts. Sometimes we can't get in and discover we have something in our pocket – some kind of attachment – that won't let us through. Sometimes we get stuck and don't know how to get back out. Sometimes we are able to go in easily, but we can't come out; sometimes we can come out, but the next day we can't go in again. One day meditation goes well, but the next day we get stuck. All sorts of things can come in the way. We learn to be observant. "What did I have in my pocket today that kept me from getting in?" We start looking and finally we say, "Oh, maybe that's it!"

On a day when he had a good meditation, I can imagine the Buddha asking himself, "What did I eat? How far did I walk? How many people was I able to help?" He would take everything into account, even physical factors. A skilled archer, he compares this to what he would ask when he hit the target. "How did I stand? What was the position of my arms? How far back did I draw the bowstring?"

Penetrating this Great Wall of Consciousness is a rare achievement. It is not impossible, but it requires an unyielding will and unified desire. Without mastering our desires, it is not possible to cross the barrier between the personal unconscious and the collective unconscious.

Most of us never even suspect that it is in our desires that all our power lies, for as our desire is, so is our will. In other words, until we develop the capacity to change our desires, we cannot have any control over our destiny.

Unifying all our desires – transforming all our passions – requires almost superhuman determination. Those who cannot resist challenge may find they are good candidates. For those who like doing what cannot be done, the transformation of desire can have a strong appeal. Even in ordinary life, if we look at those who succeed in secular fields, it's very easy to see that they have deep, unified desires to accomplish these goals.

Now the practical question is: how do we deepen the desire for nirvana? This is one of the most important questions you can ask in life. It changes your whole outlook on desire. Desire is power, and when it is perfectly unified you will be able to pierce the immense wall that separates the personal from the impersonal unconscious.

As you near this point, there comes a time in meditation when you get a distinct feeling that a door is about to open, and you are about to change levels of consciousness. You may have to wait years, but when you're burning with eagerness to discover what lies in the depths of consciousness, when you can hardly wait one more day to enter this treasure house that all scriptures say contains the pearl of untold price – as the Buddha puts it, "the jewel in the lotus of the heart" – you can be assured the door will open. Then your concentration is so complete that without warning, just for a moment, there comes what the Buddhists call a taste of "no-mind" or *bodhi*. You get a glimpse right through the stream of thought to deeper consciousness, in a blinding glimpse of pure light accompanied by a flood of joy that the Buddha says is greater than the joy of any other attainment.

It is impossible to put such experiences into words, but I can try to give you an elusive picture to the best of my small abilities of how slowly, gradually, you learn to descend into the unconscious and come up again step by step. Imagine it, then, as being like entering a vast swimming pool. First you put your toes in to test the temperature. (I am using a few light touches here, of course, so don't take this literally.) Then slowly, step by step, you go down – three feet, four feet, five feet – and the water closes over your head. There is a tremendous practical advantage to this step-by-step process: otherwise, the danger is that you might suddenly lose awareness of the body and fall, which has happened to some mystics.

Once you have reached this depth, the world within becomes as real as the world without – neither more nor less. That's very important. It's not that the world without becomes less real, but the barrier falls between the world without and the world within. This is an arbitrary barrier. There is no division between the within and the without. There is no inward life and outward life. When this barrier falls, therefore, your dependence upon events in the external world disappears. You realize that you are not dependent for your security upon any event in the world outside you – no individual, no position, no acquisition, no achievement, nothing in the external world at all. You make the discovery that all security is within, all love is within, and with that discovery you become completely independent. You rest completely on today, and because you try today to do whatever lies in your power to show your love and respect for all, you have no doubts about tomorrow.

> *All states are without self; those who realize*
> *this are freed from suffering. This is the path*
> *that leads to pure wisdom.* [279]

IN THE COLLECTIVE unconscious there is no distance between you and me; we are all there together. That's why I say at that stage there is only all. There is nothing separate. It is not the individual; it's the collective. In these depths, where you are no longer aware of your body, mind, or ego, you are no longer a separate person. You are completely united with all. The joy of it is so intense that you may find it very hard to come up to the world of separateness again. The sheer pull of this joy, the sheer draw of this universal love, has made quite a few mystics forget the world. But when you have a great desire to help people, you can use that desire to bring yourself slowly back up to the surface level. You don't lose any joy in this; the joy of helping, serving, guiding, and supporting others is equal to what you feel deep below.

Words are inadequate to describe these states of consciousness, but the Buddha assures us that they are real, as real as the dinner you had this evening. They are valid experiences which are within the reach of everyone for whom they are an overriding goal. Those who want nirvana the most, those who are prepared to give their all to this supreme goal, will attain it. This is not philosophy but experiential knowledge. It is the timeless message of India and the Buddha that ordinary people like you and me can achieve this highest state.

> More than those who hate you, more than
> all your enemies, an undisciplined mind does
> greater harm. More than your mother, more
> than your father, more than all your family,
> a well-disciplined mind does greater good.
> [42-43]

THE THINKING PROCESS has such immense momentum that even in deep meditation, concentration has the power to stop it only for an instant before it starts up again. The first glimpse of what lies beyond the mind is so momentary that it is said to take place in the twinkling of an eye. But except for great titans like the Buddha, I don't think bodhi can become a permanent state unless and until it is repeated over and over again, sometimes over a period of years. You repeat it over and over again – two moments, then three, then four. It is an agonizingly gradual process, but the joy of this experience is so intense that slowly but surely all your desires for life's lesser satisfactions merge in the deep, driving desire to do everything possible to stop the mind again.

This experience cannot last. Like a diver, you have to come up for air. But in that moment, the experience of unity has left an indelible imprint. Never again will you believe yourself a separate creature, a finite physical entity that was born to die. You know firsthand that you are inseparable from the whole of creation, and you are charged by the power of this experience to serve all life. Never again will you cling willingly to the old baggage of the mind, and once free you'll realize what a great burden you have shed.

It is important to understand that the Buddha's approach to sorrow, suffering, and illness is different from a secular approach. Instead of trying to take on problems one by one and solve them one by one, the Buddha suggests a better way. The Buddha asks, Why don't you train the mind through meditation? Then go deep within, leaving this level behind, with all its problems, addictions, bondage, and suffering. Then sorrow cannot touch you.

> *Keeping company with the immature is like*
> *going on a long journey with an enemy. The*
> *company of the wise is joyful, like reunion with*
> *one's family. Therefore, live among the wise,*
> *who are understanding, patient, responsible,*
> *and noble. Keep their company as the moon*
> *moves among the stars.* [207–208]

ON THE NIGHT the Buddha attained nirvana, when Mara found finally that all his temptations could not affect Siddhartha, he tried his most cunning strategy.

"Blessed One," he said, "you have attained nirvana, but who will believe you? No one believes in nirvana. You should stay here, rejoicing in your illumination, and never return to the world."

For the first time that night the Buddha was shaken. But only for a moment.

"No, Mara, you are mistaken. The whole world may not believe me, but there will be a few who have only a little dust in their eyes. They will try to reach the other shore."

With that answer Mara left him, and the Buddha's peace was complete.

After the final defeat of Mara, the Buddha's rapture was so great that he sat unmoving under the bodhi tree for seven days and nights. On the eighth day he left for Sarnath, near Benares. There he entered a deer park, where he delivered his first sermon, which came to be called "Setting in Motion the Wheel of the Dharma."

The Buddha was twenty-nine years old when he left home, and thirty-five when he entered nirvana. Then for forty-five years he walked the dusty roads of North India, helping kings and queens, thieves and prostitutes, farmers and merchants, rich and poor wherever he went. Gradually more and more people began to hear of him and seek his teaching. In our Indian tradition, they also came to have his *darshan* – the blessing of seeing a human being who has transcended all selfishness to become the embodiment of love, compassion, and wisdom.

And so began the world's loving response to the austere sage, a response that continues even to this day. So many wanted to be near him, to receive his teaching, and to offer their devoted assistance – because he had not abandoned them, but had returned to them from that farthest shore of nirvana.

The Buddhist scriptures tell the stories.

First is King Bimbisara, one of the Buddha's greatest disciples, who not only gave the Compassionate One a lovely grove of bamboo where he could rest and teach, but even commanded his personal physician – Jivaka, the finest doctor of the time – to take care of the Buddha. "His life is worth taking care of," he told Jivaka, "not mine. Give him all your attention."

Another man, a rich merchant called Anathapindika, also became a disciple of the Buddha at that time. He gave the Compassionate One another beautiful park, called Jetavana. So now the simple monk had two beautiful places where all could gather.

Finally, Lady Vishaka, the wife of the mayor of Savatthi, placed her jeweled tiara at the Buddha's feet, saying, "This crown belongs on your head, not on mine." The Buddha promptly exchanged the gift for a third park. So the order of monks and the sangha of householder devotees grew, and the Buddha spent his years content to travel the roads and pass the rainy seasons in one of his beloved groves, always teaching, always showing by his life what it meant to live the dharma.

◈ *The Other Shore*

ON THE FULL-MOON night in the month of May more than twenty-five hundred years ago, Prince Siddhartha awoke from his long sleep of separateness and became the Buddha, the Awakened One. The whole world was filled with joy, the Buddhist chroniclers say, and heavenly musicians gathered in the skies to fill the firmament with sweet music. Trees burst into blossom and birds sang at midnight, because when even one person crosses over into nirvana, every creature on earth receives a blessing.

The tremendous experience on the night of the Buddha's enlightenment is the foundation for everything that came afterwards, because the core of all religion is the mystical experience. Religion comes alive through the mystical experience, and so Buddhism was born on the night of the Buddha's enlightenment. D. T. Suzuki, the thoughtful Buddhist writer from Japan, says, "Mysticism is the life of religion; without it religion loses the reason of its existence – all its warm vitality is gone, all its inexpressible charms vanish, and there remains nothing but the crumbling bones and the cold ashes of death."

In light of this, we can understand why many forms of religion do not appeal to people today. No one likes collecting crumbling bones or scattering the cold ashes of death. Yet even after more than two millennia the Buddha speaks to us powerfully because his teachings rest on this supreme experience of awakening: "I reached in experience the nirvana which is unborn, unrivaled."

> *How can you describe him in human language*
> *– the Buddha, the awakened one, free from the*
> *net of desires and the pollution of passions, free*
> *from all conditioning?* [180]

IN THE LANGUAGE of the Buddha, what we call the waking state is really a dream state. As long as we live on this shore, in the world of impermanence, the Buddha says, we are asleep. The curious thing is that as long as we believe we are awake, there is nothing he can do for us. He must shake us really hard to get us to wake up out of our dream.

When I was growing up, there were dense teak forests just to the north of my village where wild animals roamed freely. A classmate of mine from that area used to tell us now and then that a cow or a goat had been carried off by a tiger during the night.

Imagine a hardworking laborer in that area who goes to the forest to collect firewood, which he carries home on his head. He has been in the forest all day, he is tired, and as soon as he has finished dinner he falls asleep – and dreams that a tiger is about to attack him. He hears the roar of the tiger, sees the creature about to pounce upon him, and he cries out in his sleep, "Help! Help!"

At this moment, imagine the Buddha entering his dream world. The villager would say, "My pulse is racing! I can't breathe!" He is terrified; he is still dreaming, still seeing the tiger. It would be absurd to tell him, "This is not a tiger. This is just a dream."

But if the Buddha can shake him out of his sleep, he will jump up quite embarrassed. "Usually I'm a courageous man," he laughs. "Why was I afraid of a tiger that was not there?"

If it is possible for someone who is asleep and dreaming of a tiger to wake up, might it then be possible to wake up from our everyday state of consciousness into a higher state of awareness? If it is possible for a dreamer to be awakened from a dream, is it not possible that you and I could wake up from the dream that money can make us secure, the hallucination that pleasure will make us happy, the nightmare that power can make us fulfilled? This is the sharp thrust of the Buddha's logic, which we can't escape.

After all, what is the proof that our waking consciousness is real except the evidence of our senses? This is exactly the proof the dreamer also adduces for the reality of his dream. How do we judge that a person is awake? He seems very busy, she has many things to attend to, so they must be awake. But isn't it the same in sleep? There are people who talk in their sleep. (Fortunately they mumble.) There are people who walk in their sleep – who get up and tiptoe to the corner without disturbing anybody, stand for ten minutes surveying the scene with wide-open eyes, and then come back, lie down, and continue to sleep. Or take another example: look at a dog while it's asleep; you may see its legs twitching as if it were running. As far as that dog is concerned, it is running on the road.

Here the Buddha is leading us to a terrifying point: how much difference is there between someone who is awake and walking about and one who is asleep and walking about? When we are acting during the day, he implies, we're just acting out our dreams – acting out the desires, motives, conflicts, and attachments in our consciousness, exactly as we do when we are asleep.

Until we wake up, in other words, we live in an illusion of life, dreaming that by making money or attaining power or possessing this person or leaving that one we can be happy. In life, just as in a dream, there is sorrow when we don't get what we want, and there is sorrow when we can't get rid of what we don't want. All this joy and sorrow passes in a reverie, lasting no longer than a dream. It shocks us when the Buddha says that such a state is not living, that people in this state have not really lived. They have been snoozing in their upper berth, dreaming, falling, then climbing back up again, dreaming, falling. Poignantly, the Buddha asks, How many times must you fall, friend, before you learn to wake yourself up and live?

All the furious activity of the mind, all our passions and conflicts and the turmoil of our desires for pleasure and profit – all this is a dream. "I'm going to fly to Acapulco," we say, "and spend the rest of my life on the beach. Then I'll be happy from morning till night." People who have tried this generally find that after a certain period the desire changes, and then there is nothing left except a big bill. It happens to all.

*It is hard to obtain human birth, harder to live
like a human being, harder still to understand
the dharma, but hardest of all to attain
nirvana.* [182]

TRAGICALLY, AS LONG as we are dreaming, we do not know that we are dreaming. I confess that I did not know. When I was a professor of English, I was dreaming on campus and getting paid for it. (My students were dreaming too.) Later, when I took to meditation, I began to wake up, little by little. It was difficult, but I had an all-consuming desire to wake up which relegated everything else to unimportance. Finally, to my amazement, I began to see that I had been dreaming, and that now I was beginning to leave the world of delusion behind.

Today I understand that dreamlike state because I remember it so well. But when people ask me to compare my life in those days to my life today, I say without exaggeration that today is a million times better, a million times richer, a million times higher, because today I am awake. This is everybody's capacity. No one should feel incapable of waking up. I do not say this from what I have read in books. In a very small way, what I say comes from personal experience.

WHEN ASKED IF the world is real, the Buddha says no. When asked if the world is unreal, the Buddha says no. Then what is the world? The Buddha says: "It is in between."

We may want to complain that the Blessed One is blowing hot and cold in the same breath, but the brilliant Buddhist philosopher Nagarjuna explains that there is relative truth and there is absolute truth.

Pointing to a group of students gathered around him in a large hall, Nagarjuna might say, "There are many people here and they are all wearing different kinds of clothes. They have been to different schools, and have taken up different jobs, and of course they have many different samskaras. Tonight at dinner all these people did justice to a good meal." So on a certain level it is true that there are many people present in the hall. That is relative truth. We can't deny it. After all, they did enjoy a good dinner; we can't say that was an illusion because a lot of substance was consumed.

But that is only relative truth. In the depths of consciousness, Nagarjuna would explain, there are not many people; there is only undivided consciousness. When we wake up, we realize that it is this unity that is real. We will know that there are not one hundred separate people in the hall. That is absolute truth.

When Nagarjuna says that on one level we are many and on the deepest level we are one, he is giving us a test for measuring what is real. Whatever changes is not real. Therefore, he says, the body has only a relative reality. If it were real in the absolute sense, it should still be here three hundred years from now. Only what never changes is real.

Sometimes in a dream I see myself going to the beach in my Volvo, just as I do during the day when I'm awake. The dream Volvo lasts just a few moments, but if I take good care of it, the daytime Volvo will last ten years or more. From Nagarjuna's point of view, however, there isn't much difference between a few moments and ten years. In that sense all the cars on the

highway are dream cars. If I come ten or twenty years later looking for them, all of them will be gone. If the Buddha were present he would say in his infinite compassion, "My dear friends,
those were dream cars. They cannot help but vanish."

A hundred years from now, all our dream cars will be gone.
We ourselves will be gone. But what the Buddha calls "the
unborn and unconditioned" will always be. This is the great discovery the Buddha asks us to make. He is asking us to wake up
from a sorrowful condition into a condition of joy beyond the
reach of change.

> There is an unborn, an unbecome, an unmade, an un-
> compounded. If there were not this unborn, unbecome,
> unmade, uncompounded, there would not be an escape
> from the born, from the become, from the made, from
> the compounded. But because there is an unborn, an
> unbecome, an unmade, an uncompounded, therefore
> there is an escape from the born, the become, the made,
> the compounded.

Our life is not unreal, but compared to the immense depth
and height we can reach we can truly call our everyday life a
dream. But through the practice of meditation, though it may
take a long, long time, we *can* wake up, just as the Buddha has
done. Then we will see that we had been using only a fraction of
our creativity and our capacity to love. Until then we are only
partially awake compared to our inborn capacity for loving all,
for living in maximum health, joy, creativity, and wisdom.

The wise understand this, and rejoice in the
wisdom of the noble ones. Meditating earnestly
and striving for nirvana, they attain the
highest joy and freedom. [22–23]

WHEN WE SEE somebody sitting with closed eyes in profound meditation, we are seeing someone who is actually waking himself up. The more the mind quiets down, the more we are awake. The more the mind is agitated, the less we are awake. And when the mind is completely still, when self-will has been extinguished and separateness has been eliminated, we see we are an integral part of the whole of life. That is what being completely awake means.

When the thought-process has been slowed to a crawl in meditation, there comes a time when – without warning – the river of the mind stops and you get a glimpse right through the mind into deeper consciousness. It is a flash of light, a flood of joy, over in an instant. Once you have experienced the state beyond the mind, you will want to do everything possible to capture that joy permanently. You will do anything, gladly give up any pleasure, to get established in that experience permanently.

The sages and saints of all the great religions say that one single taste of this experience is enough to make us long to have it always. It brings such boundless joy, such unshakable security, that we will give everything we have to be established in that state. In a brief gap between the ranks of endless thought we get a deep look into the treasures that lie in the depths of consciousness. Afterward, this glimpse haunts us because now we know that we have the capacity to traverse the mind.

Yet the thinking process has such momentum that even in deep meditation the flow of thoughts will stop only for a miraculous moment. Picture the mind as a mighty river plunging over a steep cliff, carrying everything in it over the edge. I'm told there are people who have tried to go over Niagara Falls in a barrel, which is considered to be an extreme test of human daring. Meditation is even more daring, because you are trying to do the impossible: dam the implacable torrent of the mind. Yet in meditation there are instants when the impossible is accomplished and the Niagara is frozen. Just imagine: you are in the barrel and the barrel stops. You tell Niagara Falls to stop and it does!

But the stillness is only for a fleeting moment. Every second the barrel stops, then moves, then stops again – moves, stops, moves, stops. Finally, when you reach the bottom of the falls, you say, "What's the daring in this? A barrel that stops every second is completely safe." That's what happens when thinking is slowed down almost to a standstill. The water falls, then stops; falls, then stops; falls, then stops.

After this taste of stillness in deep meditation, we do not see the world as we saw it before – so we don't live in the same world we used to live in. Even physically, leave aside metaphysically, the world is not the same. We have a glimpse that we are not a physical object but an eternal force, a permanent part of the whole. This brings such joy that the pleasures of the world pale into insignificance. It brings such security that the storms of the world cannot touch us at all. That is why we are so eager to make this experience permanent.

People are often under the impression that we can wake up one morning and find ourselves illumined. After publishing *Childe Harold's Pilgrimage,* Byron said, "I awoke one morning and found myself famous." Many people see spiritual awakening the same way, as if it could come like the sunrise. I don't want to sound a discouraging note, but it is important to understand that even in the case of spiritual giants, illumination is usually a gradual process like any other natural development. Every day, little by little, our wrong identification with the body and the other skandhas begins to weaken. Slowly, ego-identification begins to fade like the Cheshire Cat in *Alice in Wonderland*. Bit by bit the cat disappears, leaving only a smile. That's how the false ego can be made to disappear, finally leaving just the sliver of an "I" to function in life beautifully.

Yet it is true that in the case of a few extremely rare saints and sages, there is reason to believe that illumination can come all of a sudden. Ramana Maharshi became illumined when he was a boy of sixteen, and the impact was so tremendous that for a long time afterward he could not adjust himself to the world at all. It took a number of years for him to recover his balance and begin his teaching.

That is why we can be grateful that in the case of ordinary people like you and me, awakening will come just as the lotus opens its petals: gently, naturally, gracefully, so that our balance will not be disturbed.

> *That one I call a brahmin who has crossed*
> *the river difficult and dangerous to cross, and*
> *safely reached the other shore.* [414]

ONCE WE GLIMPSE the glory of the ultimate goal of nirvana, we begin to take all the difficulties of the journey in our stride. But the Buddha never wants us to forget that the way is *durga,* "a hard road," terribly difficult to traverse. Everywhere there are warnings: Difficult. Dangerous. Impossible. We should be astonished if anyone tells us the path is smooth. "How could that be?" we should protest. "Then there would be no challenge in it: no opportunity to develop, to grow, to strengthen my muscles."

Living on the surface level of consciousness, we can have no idea of the tests and trials that will come our way when we break through into the uncharted sea of the unconscious. In a sense, it is too frightening even for the imagination to contemplate, and the intellectual explanations we find in books pale into insignificance when we actually go deep into this vast, uncharted sea.

> *Blessed is the birth of the Buddha, blessed*
> *is the teaching of the dharma; blessed is the*
> *sangha, where all live in harmony.* [194]

BECAUSE THE OBSTACLES we will face at last are almost humanly impossible, in India we believe that for ordinary people like you and me the spiritual journey cannot be led from beginning to end alone. Fortunately there are forces to help us – and islands of refuge, if we but look for them. This is the meaning of an affirmation that is repeated every day by millions of people who find that devotion to the Buddha is a refuge in the stormy sea of life: "I take refuge in the Buddha, I take refuge in the dharma, I take refuge in the sangha."

Take refuge in the Buddha, the dharma, and
the sangha and you will grasp the Four Noble
Truths: suffering, the cause of suffering, the end
of suffering, and the Noble Eightfold Path that
takes you beyond suffering. That is your best
refuge, your only refuge. When you reach it, all
sorrow falls away. [190–192]

THE STORY OF Kisa Gotami touches us deeply because it is about an ordinary, unremarkable woman who was blessed to take refuge at the feet of the Compassionate One, who wiped all her tears away.

Kisa Gotami, "Gotami the delicate," is a young mother whose baby has been bitten by a cobra. Her heart broken into a thousand fragments, she comes weeping to the Buddha with the dead child in her arms. The Compassionate One, who feels her sorrow as deeply as she feels it herself, looks at her with tender eyes and asks, "What do you want me to do?"

With complete faith in the Buddha's power to move heaven and earth, she replies, "Bring my little boy back to life. I cannot live if he is dead."

His voice laden with compassion and tenderness, the Buddha replies, "Please go to the village and bring me a handful of mustard seed from any home in which there has been no death."

So Kisa Gotami goes and knocks on the door of the first home she sees. "Kind mother," she asks, "can you give me a handful of mustard seed?"

The woman at the door says, "Of course."

But then Kisa Gotami remembers the Buddha's command. "Has there been a death in your family?" she asks.

"Oh, yes, many have died here," the housewife replies. "Many people I knew as a girl have passed away in this house."

Kisa Gotami says, "Then I have to go somewhere else, because the master said I must bring mustard seed from a house in which no death has taken place."

She goes to the second home. Again, the woman at the door says she can give the handful of mustard seed. Again Kisa Gotami asks, "Have there been deaths in your home?" And this woman, too, says, "Oh, yes, some of my dear ones have gone on."

Kisa Gotami goes to house after house, and the same story is repeated again and again. Finally she reaches the last home in the village. Only then does she learn the lesson that death is universal, that there is no escaping this fate that comes to all. She returns to the Buddha, not in despair but with a deep desire to find the way beyond death.

Through the Buddha's compassion, Kisa Gotami became wise because she understood what so many never realize: that it is not possible to build our lives on anything that changes, because sooner or later – after twenty years, thirty years, forty years – death will say, "Now it's time for you to drop all these games, because I have come to collect your body."

Today there seems almost a conspiracy to pretend that there is no such thing as death, that it will come only to another home, to another person. It is a great blessing to see through this illusion. Then we don't waste time going after hollow goals like meaningless material possessions, pleasure, and fame. We seek nirvana, the island beyond death, and put everything else afterwards.

The end of suffering comes when we understand that this body is a house that was put together one day and must therefore be demolished one day. I remember when an old house in our neighborhood was torn down. I felt sad to see a gracious old home go, but I knew that was not a cause for distress. The house we occupied for nine years after returning from India was also demolished so that new apartments could be built. I was quite attached to the meditation room there. I'm sure all of us who lived there felt a sense of loss. But we are not going to spend the rest of our lives saying, "Comfort me, my house has been demolished. You don't know what heartache I have suffered."

This is strong talk, but the Compassionate Buddha declares that when you have lived wisely, made the lives of those around you better because of your days on earth, then when you find this body is no longer fit for service, where is the need to cry?

> *When a bhikshu stills his mind, he enters an*
> *empty house; his heart is full of the divine joy*
> *of the dharma. Understanding the rise and fall*
> *of the elements that make up the body, he gains*
> *the joy of immortality.* [373–374]

WHEN THE MIND is still, that is the highest state. Then you enter nirvana, where all frontiers are erased, all differences are wiped away, and the fierce thirst of separateness is quenched. Then joy comes to you, love comes to you, wisdom comes to you. Until you attain it, you cannot even imagine that you are capable of attaining that state. Only afterwards do you realize what tremendous security you have, what tremendous love you have. You enter the highest state of consciousness, which is your destiny, journey's end. You come fully into a higher mode of knowing. Instead of flashes of insight, you live permanently in the awakened state.

"An empty house" sounds negative, but it is not. This is the symbol of a mind at peace. My joy and sorrow are not the work of the movements of the planets; they are the work of my own mind, entirely the responsibility of my own mind. The whole wheel of becoming is caused by the incessant activity of the mind. If I can still my mind, therefore, I am free. I have gone beyond sorrow. The wheel of becoming, "the rise and fall of the elements," has stopped.

> *I have gone through many rounds of birth*
> *and death, looking in vain for the builder of*
> *this body. Heavy indeed is birth and death*
> *again and again! But now I have seen you,*
> *housebuilder; you shall not build this house*
> *again. Its beams are broken; its dome is*
> *shattered: self-will is extinguished; nirvana is*
> *attained.* [153–154]

THESE ARE THE immortal words the Compassionate One uttered after he attained nirvana under the bodhi tree, announcing to the world that he has discovered the cause of all our sorrows and the way to put an end to them forever.

In nirvana the prison of self-will is broken: "its beams are broken; its dome is shattered." That is the simple secret of nirvana, and more than this we need not know. Whether in the modern world or in the time of the Buddha, the essential nature of nirvana is the same, as the Buddha reveals in the perfect image of the "housebuilder" ego, which drives us on from birth to birth until we escape at last. When I extinguish all that is separate, selfish, and self-willed in me, I realize the glory of the unity of life, called dharma, "that which holds all together."

"For many, many lives," the Buddha says, "I have been looking for the builder of this house." This ego-house is a prison in which all of us serve a life sentence without even knowing it. When we believe in our separateness, we are in prison in solitary confinement, making it impossible to relate deeply to those around us and to make a worthy contribution to life.

Too often, when we go about looking for our jailer, we look outside rather than inside – to other people, to external circumstances. We do not see who has built this prison and who guards the gates so that we can never escape. The appalling truth is that eventually we come to love our jailer. We like to be propelled by self-will. We take pleasure in being prodded by the ego, and we think we are being true to ourselves in listening to the voice of our jailer.

The Buddha – even the Buddha! – confesses that he has been looking for this jailer for many, many lives. Even for him the truth did not come easily. How can the rest of us expect to see easily how we have come to live in an ego-prison where we suffer the assaults of separateness day in and day out, life after life?

When the Buddha says our ego will disappear in nirvana, naturally we find it terrifying. Our first response is to say, "No thank you. I don't want to be a zombie."

The Buddha replies, "What do you think you are now?" Then he will add, "Look at me. Am I a zombie?"

"No, you're not, Blessed One," we reply. "You're right. *We* are."

WHEN THE BUDDHA uses the term *nirvana,* he makes it clear that he is not talking about something that can be captured in thought or expressed in words, because it is a state beyond the reach of thought. It follows that almost all questions regarding nirvana are inapt.

The Buddha never allowed himself to be drawn into metaphysical controversy for a very practical reason: such questions are not relevant to the extinction of suffering. Such questions, he would say, are a waste of time, and he warned his followers not to allow doctrine and dogma to distract from the path to the supreme goal. This is why the Buddha paid so little attention to intellectual arguments and the endless debates of the philosophers of his day.

Even in the Buddha's day there were many, many people who asked him to describe nirvana. Again, the document called *The Questions of King Milinda* sets the scene. Though he was a king, Milinda spent many fruitful hours asking Nagasena to elucidate the fundamental teachings of the Buddha. Naturally, the discussion finally came to nirvana, and King Milinda was not able to understand what nirvana is, nor was Nagasena able to explain it to his satisfaction. After a frustrating debate Milinda asked, "But what is this nirvana like, Nagasena? Give me a simile."

Nagasena, very practical in his illustrations, said, "Great King, is there something called 'wind'?"

"Of course," Milinda answered, "Surely there is such a thing as wind."

"Will Your Majesty show me the wind?" Nagasena replies. "Can you tell me its color? Is it long or short? Thick or thin?"

His Majesty smiles a royal smile and says, "One cannot point to the wind like that. You cannot grasp the wind with the hand. Nevertheless, my dear Nagasena, there *is* such a thing as wind."

"Well," Nagasena answers, "if one cannot point to the wind and say whether it is black or white, tall or short, thick or thin, one might be tempted to conclude that there is no wind at all."

"But my dear Nagasena, how can you say that? I know there is such a thing as wind!"

"Just so, Your Majesty, there is nirvana," Nagasena says quietly. "But one cannot point to it, saying it is this or it is that. One cannot say it is one thing or the other."

Being a fair-minded gentleman who enjoys debating, His Majesty replies, "Very good, Nagasena! Clear is the simile; convincing is the argument. So it is, and so I accept it. There is nirvana."

It's a beautiful story. Everybody believes in wind. Even skeptics are convinced that wind is real because its effects are real: it blows down trees, brings in storms, and howls in the night. Similarly, the effects of nirvana are real. Everybody benefits from coming in contact with a person who has attained nirvana. Everybody can feel the benefit of it, everybody can see the beauty of it: not only those who lead the spiritual life but even those who do not; not only people who believe in the Buddha, but people who haven't even heard of him. That is the wonderful conclusion we can draw from this remarkable story of King Milinda and Nagasena.

To follow the Buddha's path, it is important to understand that the moments of stillness are what count, not intellectual views. Until we have this experience of stillness for ourselves, discussion of nirvana is only an intellectual exercise. Therefore, when asked a purely theoretical question, the Buddha would neither affirm nor deny it. If you ask him, "Is there God?" he would say, "Maybe." If you ask him to deny God, he would say, "I am not prepared to do that."

One of the strangest characters in the Buddhist sutras, which are not lacking in eccentrics, is a man whose name means "one whose hair is like a blanket." This fellow must have had a lot of hair. One day, the Buddha was talking about him with Ananda, his dear companion. "Ananda," he says, "this fellow with hair like a blanket once asked me, 'Is there a Self?'"

Ananda looks alert and says, "Blessed One, what did you answer?"

"I answered nothing."

This is delicious. This is the Buddha in one of his playful, teasing moods. For many, many questions like this, the most the Buddha would say is simply, "This is an unprofitable question." What he is trying to say is, "You are physically oriented, egocentrically oriented; how can you grasp that which requires an entirely different mode of understanding?" If a questioner persisted, the Buddha could pretend to be mildly annoyed.

In books on Buddhism speculative questions are often asked, such as "Is there eternal life?" or "Is the self present after nirvana?" These questions cannot be asked. If I ask, "Will I continue to exist after attaining nirvana?" I am asking the first part of the question standing in separateness – "Will I" – and then in the second part of the question I am standing in nirvana. A good intellect can grasp the absurdity. The Buddha will say, "First come out of your sleeping state. Then let's talk."

To understand the mystics of any religion, the intellect is of little value. In order to understand the Buddha, we have to become like the Buddha. We cannot measure an illumined man or woman because we don't have the right kind of tape. I have a friend who is a carpenter; when he is working he keeps a folding ruler in his pocket and a tape measure on his belt. That's all right for measuring walls, doors, and windows, but there is no instrument long enough to measure the Buddha, to measure nirvana, because they are beyond measure.

To know why the Buddha acts in a particular way, you have to be the Buddha. You have to have awakened yourself from the lowest state of consciousness to the highest. Not even the gods or angels, the scriptures say, can know the way of the Buddha. How then can ordinary human beings understand?

On more than one occasion, a particularly persistent disciple might go on asking, "What state are you in, then? I want to know that."

The Buddha easily parried the question. "There is no measuring of one who has disappeared; there is no way whereby one might know of him that he is not." He has reached the other shore. His "I" is not there, his private individuality is not there, so what is there to be measured?

On many occasions he warned the monks not to dip the string of thought into the infinite ocean, or break their heads against the mountain, because trying to fathom the unfathomable is useless, unprofitable.

BECAUSE IT IS so hard to understand the man or woman who has reached the other shore, the final verses in the last chapter of the Dhammapada are precious. Here a few simple words describe the illumined man or woman as the real brahmin, not in the sense of those belonging to the highest caste because of birth, but those who are revered because they have achieved life's supreme goal.

> *That one I call a brahmin whose way no one*
> *can know. Such a one lives free from past and*
> *future, free from decay and death.* [420]

SUCH A PERSON is beyond compare. He or she is perfect, which is a concept foreign to our human understanding. For a long, long time, you and I struggle to replace bad habits with good habits. It is a tiresome task, the work of the first part of the spiritual journey, in which all bad habits must be replaced by good habits one by one. As we struggle at this task, it is impossible even to conceive of the ultimate stage, after enlightenment, when we have no habits at all.

The Buddha has no habits, no samskaras, either good or bad. It is an amazing statement, but the mystics of all traditions confirm what the Buddha says: we become free, and in becoming free we become spontaneous. I have been asked whether it isn't blasphemous to talk about the enlightened person as beyond all that is good as well as all that is bad. It isn't easy for us – no, it isn't possible for us – to understand that for a Buddha, a completely enlightened person, a harmful thought is unimaginable. He or she cannot do harm to anyone. Perfect enlightenment is incapable of harm; perfect love is incapable of wrong.

That one I call a brahmin who is fearless,
heroic, unshakable, a great sage who has
conquered death and attained life's goal. [422]

THE BUDDHA USES the word *hero* here for those who
have won the great battle against themselves. These are the people who are truly victorious. No adversary can shake them; no
force on earth can make them swerve from their path or lose
their love.

Just as soldiers coming home from war were received with
brass bands, banners, and banquets, the Buddha is implying, that
is how we should honor the illumined man or woman who has
waged the long, fierce war against human weaknesses and won. It
is to people like this that the songs should be sung and the med-
als given, for they are the true heroes, the bravest of the brave.

I have never met any human being as fearless as my grandmother. Even Mahatma Gandhi, you may remember, had to get
over all kinds of fears: ghosts, snakes, even being alone in the
dark. I don't think my granny was ever afraid of anything or
anybody – not of any circumstance or any force on earth.

Whenever there was any threat in my village, everyone in our
home used to come to my granny. During the days of the Mus-
lim rebellion in Kerala, even some of my uncles came to her and
said, "Come stay with us. We are brave, but we have fear in our
hearts. When you are close to us, there is no fear at all."

When I was a boy, I would often ask my granny questions and
listen to her stories in the evening. I would come home after
soccer deliciously exhausted and lie down on our bamboo cot
with my head resting on her lap. It was heaven for me when I

was a boy. Once I asked her, "Granny, how can I become fearless like you?" She said, "One day you will."

I don't think I believed it. Even later, when I was at the university and had overcome many childhood fears, I wouldn't have called myself a brave man. I saw many famous people in those days, but I used to tell my granny that I had never seen anybody so completely fearless as she was. "I have seen people from Europe and America," I would tell her, "but I have never seen anybody without a sense of fear except you."

With all humility, today I can say I'm just like my grandmother. I don't have any fear, not only of this life but of what is in store after death. Today I know I can go deeper than any fear, and from that depth I can pluck that fear out by the root and throw it away. That is the discovery we make in deepest meditation, and it is one of the grandest results of reaching the other shore.

> *Brahmins have reached the end of the way;*
> *they have crossed the river of life. All that they*
> *had to do is done: they have become one with*
> *all life.* [423]

THOSE WHO HAVE achieved nirvana leave all doubts behind. The intellect is a heckler; that is its job. But when nirvana is reached, the intellect at last must fall silent. At that time all doubts leave us, all reservations are left behind. In nirvana all the files of doubts that we have accumulated are thrown into the fire. Afterwards, the whole world can say there is no such thing as nirvana and we'll say, "Thank you, I disagree." All science can say nirvana is a myth, but the illumined man or woman will not be swayed.

Those who are awake have done what needs to be done. They have done their job, finished the task that life has set for them. They have gone home.

Overcoming every obstacle that is the human legacy of millions of years of evolution, on that supreme night of awakening the Buddha fulfilled his human destiny. To put it simply, he seized the most important prize in life – most important because until we enter nirvana, we will come into this life again and again until we do what we have to do.

According to the Hindu and Buddhist sages, we have been making a new body in every life – life after life, again and again, for millions of years. Like welders in an auto shop, we have our body shops, and in every life we put on our earmuffs and strike sparks off, customizing the physical skandha to our desires. Until we enter nirvana this process will go on for a million years, and then another million years, driven by desire – driven by the mind. But once we learn to change our desires, once we learn to turn negative emotions into positive, we are free. Then, the Buddha says, we have reached our last body. When we have obtained complete mastery over our actions, words, and thoughts – when our hearts are full of love for everybody, all countries, all creatures, all of creation – there are no more selfish desires to be fulfilled, no more need to be reborn.

Health is the best gift, contentment the best
wealth, trust the best kinsman, nirvana the
greatest joy. Drink the nectar of the dharma in
the depths of meditation, and become free from
fear and sin. [204–205]

THIS IS ONE of the most compelling of the Buddha's declarations: *nibbanam param sukham,* "Nirvana is the greatest joy."

When you have erased all self-will, gone beyond the concept of "I, me, and mine," you are in nirvana, the state of joy. How paradoxical it sounds! Yet, on the strength of my small experience, I can tell you that when you are able to extinguish your self-will and embrace all those around you in love, you'll see that nirvana is not extinction; it is the blessed state of love for all.

In the Dhammapada the words to describe nirvana are precise and practical. Nirvana is all that is good, all that is joy – a million times greater than any worldly joy. As a prince, the Buddha was well acquainted with the pleasures and luxuries of life, but when he entered into nirvana, the joy was so intense that his body could not bear it. His senses, his private personality, could not bear the joy. Body, mind, and ego fainted away as he sat transfixed to the spot under the bodhi tree, lost in the joy that knows no limit. One taste of this joy would ravish us. The mystics and saints of all religions say, "How could I have ever thought I was awake when I tasted only a millionth part of this joy, felt only a millionth part of this love, lived only a millionth part of this life?"

The love that we feel in nirvana is a million times more than the love we can have in even the most loving of human relationships. Established in nirvana, the Buddha sees life as one, and therefore he loves all life, from the smallest creature to all human beings, with a deep desire to help and serve all. Every morning with a joy and love that knows no bounds, he looks forward to the dawn for another glorious day in which to help others cross the sea of life.

When you have even just a glimpse of the other shore, you will know that there is nothing the world can give you, no material possession or pleasure that can add to your joy. You live in the kingdom of joy, which sorrow cannot touch – on a deeper, richer level where the problems of the world of impermanence cannot reach you. For such a person, personal sorrow has no latchkey. Hatred, jealousy, resentment, malice, cannot enter such a person's mind. There is no question of how to deal with emotions like these, because they cannot enter at all.

The final verse of the Dhammapada contains a description of the Buddha which almost defies translation. The literal translation is "one who is able to see heaven and hell at the same time": that is, one who is able to live in complete joy but always remembers that there are many around who are in sorrow. Perhaps this is a warning not to bask in the joy and get caught in it like a bee in honey – the same honey that it has made. There have been a few figures in mysticism who unfortunately have been submerged in their own infinite joy and forgotten the suffering world, denying it the great love and service they could render.

The Buddha has one eye on eternity because he knows he was never born and will never die. But at the same time, he knows that ordinary human beings do think – just as he used to think – that they are the body, the mind, and the ego, so they are born to die. He is able to understand our needs, problems, and difficulties, but the solution he offers us is from eternity – from the world beyond time, space, and causality.

> Like the flight of birds in the sky, the path of
> the selfless is hard to follow. They have no
> possessions, but live on alms in a world of
> freedom.
>
> Like the flight of birds in the sky, their path is
> hard to follow. With their senses under control,
> temperate in eating, they know the meaning of
> freedom. [92–93]

NOW WE COME to one of the most magical words in Buddhism, *shunyata*. Wherever students of the Buddha gather they cannot help talking about shunyata, which comes from the Sanskrit word *shunya* meaning "a zero, a void, an emptiness." The concept of zero was first discovered in India, and perhaps the Buddhist idea of emptiness could have come only from a culture in which the mathematical zero had first been used.

Ultimate reality, the Buddha is telling us, is opposed to anything we know. It is opposed to anything we can think of, anything we can say. Therefore it is called shunyata, "emptiness," and can be understood only through the experience of nirvana. Again and again the Buddhist philosopher Nagarjuna refuses to allow any words to describe the highest truth, because he knows the utter inadequacy of words. Finally, he allows that the word *shunyata* can be used, but he adds, "Reality cannot be called emptiness or non-emptiness, or both or neither, but in order to indicate it, it is called emptiness."

Nagarjuna just wouldn't allow any easy teachings about reality, about nirvana, or about the Self. "Although the doctrine of 'Self' is taught," he says, "and the doctrine of 'no self' is also taught, no Self or non-self whatsoever has ever been taught by the Buddha." This is the teaching of Nagarjuna, who says it is possible to be deluded by a belief in the separate existence of things and equally possible to be deluded by a belief in emptiness. Both are a net of ignorance, but the ignorance is harder to break for one who is caught in a wrong belief in emptiness or "no self." Only in nirvana do we see the truth and become free. Words, concepts, and the intellect can never release us from suffering, can never bring us freedom.

Some Buddhists who found the word *shunyata* unhelpful used an even more ineffable word, *tathata*, to try to express the inexpressible. Perhaps their students told them, "We can't grasp this shunyata," so these teachers spoke of "suchness": "that which is such as it is." This was their teaching: if you want to find the Unconditioned, find "that which is such as it is."

Even more powerful are the words of the Heart Sutra: *Gaté gaté paragaté parasamgaté bodhi svaha!* "Gone, gone, gone beyond, all gone beyond, awakened, wonderful!" Gone beyond words, gone beyond concepts, gone beyond the conditioned. Awakened! Wonderful! Such words could have been uttered only by a man or woman amazed in the face of the wonder of nirvana.

*They make holy wherever they dwell, in village
or forest, on land or at sea. With their senses
at peace and minds full of joy, they make the
forests holy.* [98–99]

THAT PLACE IS beautiful beyond expression where an awakened man or woman lives. This is the true source of beauty, unknown to us in our daily lives. Often what we consider beauty is a quality lent by external art. But even the most beautiful work of art cannot come anywhere near the resplendent beauty, the goodness beyond measure, the love beyond all expression, which a man or woman who has attained this shining goal radiates all around. It lights our path, dispels the darkness from our lives, and therefore that place – whether forest, village, or city – is beautiful where dwell those who have realized the dharma and practice it.

The Buddha does not say that the awakened person must live away from life, away "from the madding crowd's ignoble strife." Such people may live in the midst of others because that is where the need is greatest. They can be completely illumined and still live like Tom, Dick, and Harry. They can go to the market, to the theater, to the ice cream parlor, and still be completely awake, which is an extraordinarily difficult art.

The Buddha did not achieve nirvana and then settle down in a hermitage with a sign in front saying Keep Out. He went out into the world to live actively, working, serving, and teaching until the last day of his life. He worked not only for the sake of his family, who became his disciples, but for all. Villagers and merchants, the wealthy and the poor, men and women of all ages and all walks of life – all came to him to learn that death is not inevitable and we are not condemned to a meaningless world of relentless change. Everyone came to him to learn how the deepest human passions could be transfused, transformed, into tremendous power for good.

> *That one I call a brahmin who has found his*
> *heaven, free from selfish desire, free from every*
> *impurity. Wanting nothing at all, doubting*
> *nothing at all, master of both body and mind,*
> *such a one has gone beyond time and death.*
> [410–411]

FOR SUCH A person there is no more need to return, for they have "gone beyond." Once we wake ourselves up, there is no need to return. But we may be given the opportunity to come again, to join again with those who have helped us and with those we can serve. If we come, we come to serve the world as *bodhisattvas*, "those whose essence is illumination." They have no more need to be reborn, they have received their last body, but their love has become so boundless that they may say, "I'd like to go again, be born again, live with people again, so that through my life, my love, and my service, I can show those around me how to end their sorrow and cross the river of life."

Those who aspire to this ideal, who have lived together and practiced spiritual disciplines together, can come back to join together in a new life. Just because this body is shed, life is not at an end. Even after you shed your physical body, the love in your heart, which is not physical, will continue. Your pure consciousness, not limited by time and space, will continue, so that you will be able to come back in a new body to be united with those you have loved and who love you, in life after life.

This is the ideal of romance: those who love deeply are going to be together again. Your romance goes on and on and on. This realization removes all fear of death from your heart. It is very difficult, in fact impossible, to put this experience into words, but over a period of many years, as my meditation deepened and I went far below the surface level of consciousness, I too made this discovery of those who have crossed the river of life: immortality comes and embraces you.

This is the message of all the great scriptures, but although I had read the scriptures before I began to meditate, like everybody else I had not the slightest doubt that every human being, every living creature, has to die. I too believed that death is inevitable, that dust must return to dust. Only after I "reached the end of the way" was I able to say along with Longfellow, "'Dust thou art, to dust returnest' was not spoken of the soul."

When we make this discovery, the consequences are tremendous. First, there is no longer fear of the passage of time, which takes so heavy a toll particularly during the second half of life. Even a little experience of rising above the body, a little suspension of the ego, can release us from great fears.

Second, when you no longer believe you are the body, you are not burdened by the weight of it. Your steps become lighter, your back gets straighter; you feel almost that you are floating on the clouds, even though your feet are on the ground. There is a buoyancy inside that enables you to float through life despite all the storms that may blow.

Third, the barrier between you and others goes. As long as I believe obsessively that I am this physical body, I cannot help looking upon others as apart from me. When body-consciousness dies I find there is no barrier between me and you, between me and any other creature, because I see – experientially, in the very depths of my consciousness – that all life is an indivisible whole, which can never be cut up into parts.

The Buddha teaches that our next life is not dependent upon chance or fate. No outside force dictates it; it is dependent entirely on us. As we live today, so will our life be tomorrow. As we live in this life, so will our life be next time. This is the joy of the Buddha's message: take your life in your hands, learn to practice meditation, make your mode of thinking selfless, make your mind secure, extend your love to embrace all.

That is the law the Buddha calls dharma. Whether we call it worship or simply serving, the highest expression of dharma is self-sacrifice. It is very, very difficult to get over the delusion that by going after profit and pleasure we can become happy. I too had that delusion, but through the infinite love of my teacher I was able to awaken from that fantasy. Today, with all the humility at my disposal, I can repeat the words of the Buddha, "I am the happiest mortal in the world; there is no one happier than I." This is a statement every one of us can begin to repeat for ourselves. It is arduous, it takes a long time, and it requires a deeper mode of knowing brought into play through meditation, but all of us are capable of this realization.

FOR ME, THE most beautiful statue of the Buddha is in Ceylon. It is a moving representation of his last moments, lying on his side as he speaks to Ananda and the gathered monks. The Buddha came to the end of his mortal life in his eightieth year, still teaching, still walking the dusty roads of India. When he reached the village of Kushinara, feeling ill, he turned to Ananda and said, "Let me lie down under this tree."

So compassionate, so serene, the Buddha tells the heartbroken Ananda that he should not grieve. His words are addressed to all of us. "It may be, Ananda, that some of you may think my words have come to an end, that you have a teacher no longer. But you should not think so. For the dharma I have proclaimed will be your teacher when I am gone."

Then he continued. "It may be that one of you has a doubt about the Buddha, the dharma, or the sangha. So ask me, friends!"

But the monks were silent. The Buddha asked a second time and a third, but still all were silent. Finally, Ananda murmured, "It is marvelous, yet all have understood the teaching, Blessed One."

"You speak out of your great love for me, and from your faith," the Buddha replied, "but it is true, Ananda: each one here understands the dharma and will cross the river in this very life."

Then the Tathagata delivered his final words. "Listen: All compounded things, all experiences, all phenomena by their very nature decay and die. Work out your salvation with diligence. Through earnestness you will attain the goal."

Then he entered into deep meditation, deeper and deeper, and entered the ultimate state.

"The Blessed One has passed away!" cried Ananda.

"No, friend Ananda, the Blessed One has not passed away," the other monks replied. "He has entered the final nirvana,

◇ Selected Verses

This is a list of all selected verses used in this book,
in verse number order.

[1] *Our life is shaped by our mind; we become what*
we think. Suffering follows an evil thought as the
wheels of a cart follow the oxen that draw it. (p. 182)

[2] *Our life is shaped by our mind; we become what*
we think. Joy follows a pure thought like a shadow
that never leaves. (p. 183)

[7–8] *As a strong wind blows down a weak tree,*
Mara the Tempter overwhelms weak people who,
eating too much and working too little, are caught in
the frantic pursuit of pleasure. As the strongest wind
cannot shake a mountain, Mara cannot shake those
who are self–disciplined and full of faith. (p. 89)

[13–14] *As rain seeps through an ill-thatched hut,
passion will seep through an untrained mind. As rain
cannot seep through a well-thatched hut, passion
cannot seep through a well-trained mind. (p. 58)*

[15–16] *Those who are selfish suffer here and
hereafter; they suffer in both worlds from the results
of their own actions. But those who are selfless
rejoice here and rejoice hereafter. They rejoice in both
worlds from the results of their own actions. (p. 167)*

[21] *Be vigilant and go beyond death. If you lack
vigilance, you cannot escape death. Those who strive
earnestly will go beyond death; those who do not can
never come to life. (p. 51)*

[22–23] *The wise understand this, and rejoice in the
wisdom of the noble ones. Meditating earnestly and
striving for nirvana, they attain the highest joy and
freedom. (p. 226)*

[24–25] *If you meditate earnestly, pure in mind and
kind in deeds, leading a disciplined life in harmony
with the dharma, you will grow in glory. If you
meditate earnestly, through spiritual disciplines you
can make an island for yourself that no flood can
overwhelm. (p. 60, 198)*

[29–30] *Earnest among those who are indolent,*
awake among those who slumber, the wise advance
like a racehorse, leaving others behind. It was
through earnest effort that Indra became lord of the
gods. The earnest are always respected, the indolent
never. (p. 53)

[31–32] *The earnest spiritual aspirant, fearing sloth,*
advances like a fire, burning all fetters. Such seekers
will never fall back: they are nearing nirvana. (p. 49)

[33] *As an archer aims an arrow, the wise aim their*
restless thoughts, hard to aim, hard to restrain.
(p. 187)

[35–36] *Hard it is to train the mind, which goes*
where it likes and does what it wants. But a trained
mind brings health and happiness. The wise can
direct their thoughts, subtle and elusive, wherever
they choose: a trained mind brings health and
happiness. (p. 190)

[40] *Remember, this body is like a fragile clay pot.*
Make your mind a fortress and conquer Mara with
the weapon of wisdom. Guard your conquest always.
(p. 72)

[42–43] *More than those who hate you, more than all your enemies, an undisciplined mind does greater harm. More than your mother, more than your father, more than all your family, a well-disciplined mind does greater good.* (p. 214)

[50] *Do not give your attention to what others do or fail to do; give it to what you do or fail to do.* (p. 73)

[60] *Long is the night to those who are awake; long is the road to those who are weary. Long is the cycle of birth and death to those who know not the dharma.* (p. 132)

[62] *They think, "These children are mine; this wealth is mine." They cannot even call themselves their own, much less their children or wealth.* (p. 121)

[71] *As fresh milk needs time to curdle, a selfish deed takes time to bring sorrow in its wake. Like fire smoldering under the ashes, slowly does it burn the immature.* (p. 152)

[85–86] *Few are those who reach the other shore; most people keep running up and down this shore. But those who follow the dharma, when it has been*

*well taught, will reach the other shore, hard to reach,
beyond the power of death. (p. 24)*

[87–89] *They leave darkness behind and follow
the light. They give up home and leave pleasure
behind. Calling nothing their own, they purify their
hearts and rejoice. Well trained in the seven fields
of enlightenment, their senses disciplined and free
from attachments, they live in freedom, full of light.
(p. 113)*

[92–93] *Like the flight of birds in the sky, the path of
the selfless is hard to follow. They have no possessions,
but live on alms in a world of freedom. Like the flight
of birds in the sky, their path is hard to follow. With
their senses under control, temperate in eating, they
know the meaning of freedom. (p. 245)*

[98–99] *They make holy wherever they dwell, in
village or forest, on land or at sea. With their senses
at peace and minds full of joy, they make the forests
holy. (p. 247)*

[103] *One who conquers himself is greater than
another who conquers a thousand times a thousand
men on the battlefield. (p. 93)*

[104–105] *Be victorious over yourself and not over others. When you attain victory over yourself, not even the gods can turn it into defeat. (p. 90)*

[114–115] *One day's glimpse of the deathless state is better than a hundred years of life without it. One day's glimpse of dharma is better than a hundred years of life without it. (p. 210)*

[121–122] *Let no one think lightly of evil and say to himself, "Sorrow will not come to me." Little by little a person becomes evil, as a pot is filled by drops of water. Let no one think lightly of good and say to himself, "Joy will not come to me." Little by little a person becomes good, as a pot is filled by drops of water. (p. 153)*

[126] *Some are born again. Those caught in evil ways go to a state of intense suffering; those who have done good go to a state of joy. But the pure in heart enter nirvana. (p. 161)*

[131–132] *If, hoping to be happy, you strike at others who also seek happiness, you will be happy neither here nor hereafter. If, hoping to be happy, you do not strike at others who are also seeking happiness, you will be happy here and hereafter. (p. 147)*

[135] *As a cowherd with his staff drives cows to fresh fields, old age and death lead all creatures to new lives. (p. 181)*

[141–142] *Going about with matted hair, without food or bath, sleeping on the ground smeared with dust, or sitting motionless – no amount of penance can help a person whose mind is not purified. But one whose mind is serene and chaste, whose senses are controlled and whose life is nonviolent – these are true brahmins, true monks, even if they wear fine clothes. (p. 192)*

[144] *Be like a well-trained horse, swift and spirited, and go beyond sorrow through faith, meditation, and energetic practice of the dharma. (p. 87, 185)*

[153–154] *I have gone through many rounds of birth and death, looking in vain for the builder of this body. Heavy indeed is birth and death again and again! But now I have seen you, housebuilder; you shall not build this house again. Its beams are broken; its dome is shattered: self-will is extinguished; nirvana is attained. (p. 233)*

[157] *If you hold yourself dear, guard yourself diligently. Keep vigil during one of the three watches of the night. (p. 80)*

[168–169] *Wake up! Don't be lazy. Follow the right path, avoid the wrong. You will be happy here as well as hereafter. (p. 49)*

[170–171] *Look on the world as a bubble; look on it as a mirage. Then the King of Death cannot even see you. Come look at this world! Is it not like a painted royal chariot? The wise see through it, but not the immature. (p. 32)*

[172–173] *When those who are foolish become wise, they give light to the world like the full moon breaking through the clouds. When their good deeds overcome the bad, they give light to the world like the moon breaking free from behind the clouds. (p. 180)*

[178] *Better than ruling this world, better than attaining the realm of the gods, better than being lord of all the worlds, is one step taken on the path to nirvana. (p. 48, 157)*

[180] *How can you describe him in human language – the Buddha, the awakened one, free from the net of desires and the pollution of passions, free from all conditioning? (p. 220)*

[182] *It is hard to obtain human birth, harder to live like a human being, harder still to understand the dharma, but hardest of all to attain nirvana. (p. 223)*

[185] *Do not find fault with others, do not injure others, but live in accordance with the dharma. Be moderate in eating and sleeping, and meditate on the highest. This sums up the teaching of the Buddhas. (p. 75)*

[190–192] *Take refuge in the Buddha, the dharma, and the sangha and you will grasp the Four Noble Truths: suffering, the cause of suffering, the end of suffering, and the Noble Eightfold Path that takes you beyond suffering. That is your best refuge, your only refuge. When you reach it, all sorrow falls away. (p. 42, 230)*

[194] *Blessed is the birth of the Buddha, blessed is the teaching of the dharma; blessed is the sangha, where all live in harmony. (p. 229)*

[197] *Let us live in joy, never hating those who hate us. Let us live in freedom, without hatred even among those who hate. (p. 119)*

[199–200] *Let us live in joy, never attached among those who are selfishly attached. Let us live in freedom even among those who are bound by selfish attachments. Let us live in joy, never hoarding things among those who hoard. Let us live in growing joy like the bright gods. (p. 115, 141)*

[204–205] *Health is the best gift, contentment the best wealth, trust the best kinsman, nirvana the greatest joy. Drink the nectar of the dharma in the depths of meditation, and become free from fear and sin. (p. 243)*

[207–208] *Keeping company with the immature is like going on a long journey with an enemy. The company of the wise is joyful, like reunion with one's family. Therefore, live among the wise, who are understanding, patient, responsible, and noble. Keep their company as the moon moves among the stars. (p. 85, 215)*

[212] *Selfish attachment brings suffering; selfish attachment brings fear. Be detached, and you will be free from suffering and fear. (p. 102)*

[219–220] *As your family and friends receive you with joy when you return from a long journey, so will your good deeds receive you when you go from this life to the next, where they will be waiting for you with joy like your kinsmen. (p. 175)*

[221] *Give up anger, give up pride, and free yourself from worldly bondage. No sorrow can befall those who never try to possess people and things as their own. (p. 131)*

[223] *Conquer anger through gentleness, unkindness through kindness, greed through generosity, and falsehood by truth. (p. 160)*

[226] *Those who are vigilant, who train their minds day and night and strive continually for nirvana, enter the state of peace beyond all selfish passions. (p. 96)*

[252–253] *It is easy to see the faults of others; we winnow them like chaff. It is hard to see our own; we hide them as a gambler hides a losing draw. But when one keeps dwelling on the faults of others, his own compulsions grow worse, making it harder to overcome them. (p. 74)*

[274–275] *This is the path; there is no other that leads to the purification of the mind. Follow this path and conquer Mara. This path will lead to the end of suffering. This is the path I made known after the arrows of sorrow fell away. (p. 208)*

[277] *All created things are transitory; those who realize this are freed from suffering. This is the path that leads to pure wisdom. (p. 33)*

[279] *All states are without self; those who realize this are freed from suffering. This is the path that leads to pure wisdom. (p. 38, 213)*

[290] *If one who enjoys a lesser happiness beholds a greater one, let him leave aside the lesser to gain the greater. (p. 98)*

[291] *Don't try to build your happiness on the unhappiness of others. You will be enmeshed in a net of hatred. (p. 134)*

[296] *The disciples of Gautama are wide awake and vigilant, with their thoughts focused on the Buddha day and night. (p. 81)*

[297–298] *The disciples of Gautama are wide awake and vigilant, absorbed in the dharma day and night. The disciples of Gautama are wide awake and vigilant, with their thoughts focused on the sangha day and night. (p. 106)*

[301] *The disciples of Gautama are wide awake and vigilant, rejoicing in meditation day and night. (p. 81)*

[302] *It is hard to leave the world and hard to live in it, painful to live with the worldly and painful to be a wanderer. Reach the goal; you will wander and suffer no more. (p. 57)*

[311] *As a blade of kusha grass can cut the finger when it is wrongly held, asceticism practiced without discrimination can send one on the downward course. (p. 70)*

[312–313] *An act performed carelessly, a vow not kept, a code of chastity not strictly observed: these things bring little reward. If anything is worth doing, do it with all your heart. A half-hearted ascetic covers himself with more and more dust. (p. 67)*

[314] *Refrain from evil deeds, which cause suffering later. Perform good deeds, which can cause no suffering. (p. 149)*

[315] *Guard yourself well, both within and without, like a well-defended fort. Don't waste a moment, for wasted moments send you on the downward course. (p. 56)*

[322] *Mules are good animals when trained; even better are well-trained Sind horses and great elephants. Best among men is one with a well-trained mind. (p. 185)*

[327] *Be vigilant; guard your mind against negative thoughts. Pull yourself out of bad ways as an elephant raises itself out of the mud. (p. 64)*

[328] *If you find a friend who is good, wise, and loving, walk with him all the way and overcome all dangers. (p. 124)*

[331] *It is good to have friends when friendship is mutual. Good deeds are friends at the time of death. But best of all is going beyond sorrow. (p. 124)*

[334] *The compulsive urges of the thoughtless grow like a creeper. They jump like a monkey from one life to another, looking for fruit in the forest. (p. 177)*

[338] *As a tree, though cut down, recovers and grows if its roots are not destroyed, suffering will come to you more and more if these compulsive urges are not extinguished. (p. 177)*

[354] *There is no gift better than the gift of the dharma, no gift more sweet, no gift more joyful. It puts an end to cravings and the sorrow they bring. (p. 44)*

[369] *Bhikshu, empty your boat! It will go faster. Cast out greed and hatred and reach nirvana. (p. 109)*

[372] *There can be no meditation for those who are not wise, and no wisdom for those who do not meditate. Growing in wisdom through meditation, you will surely be close to nirvana. (p. 197)*

[373–374] *When a bhikshu stills his mind, he enters an empty house; his heart is full of the divine joy of the dharma. Understanding the rise and fall of the elements that make up the body, he gains the joy of immortality. (p. 232)*

[379–380] *Raise yourself by your own efforts; be your own critic. Thus self–reliant and vigilant, you will live in joy. Be your own master and protector. Train your mind as a merchant trains his horse. (p. 55)*

[383] *Cross the river bravely; conquer all your passions. Go beyond the world of fragments and know the deathless ground of life. (p. 88)*

[394–395] *What use is matted hair? What use is a deerskin on which to sit for meditation if your mind still seethes with lust? Saffron robe and outward show do not make a brahmin, but training of the mind and senses through practice of meditation. (p. 189)*

[410–411] *That one I call a brahmin who has found his heaven, free from selfish desire, free from every impurity. Wanting nothing at all, doubting nothing*

*at all, master of both body and mind, such a one has
gone beyond time and death. (p. 248)*

[414] *That one I call a brahmin who has crossed
the river difficult and dangerous to cross, and safely
reached the other shore. (p. 228)*

[420] *That one I call a brahmin whose way no one
can know. Such a one lives free from past and future,
free from decay and death. (p. 239)*

[422] *That one I call a brahmin who is fearless,
heroic, unshakable, a great sage who has conquered
death and attained life's goal. (p. 240)*

[423] *Brahmins have reached the end of the way;
they have crossed the river of life. All that they had to
do is done: they have become one with all life.
(p. 241)*

◈ *Glossary*

IN THIS VOLUME the Sanskrit form is used for most Buddhist names and terms because these are usually more familiar to English readers, but the Pali form may be used in some cases.

adharma [*a* "not"; *dharma* "law, righteousness"] Whatever is against dharma; whatever violates the eternal law of dharma.

Ajatashatru A king of Magadha who was a contemporary of the Buddha. Ajatashatru came to the throne when he imprisoned his father, Bimbisara, but he later repented his cruelty and became a follower of the Buddha.

Ananda A principal disciple of the Buddha who was his loving attendant. Ananda memorized many of the Buddha's teachings and recited them at the First Buddhist Council.

Anathapindika A wealthy merchant who was a prominent householder disciple of the Buddha.

anatta [Pali, from Skt. *an* "not"; *atma* "self"] The teaching that all things are "without a self" and therefore impermanent. Because all things in the world of change are anatta, cultivating self-will leads to unhappiness.

Angulimala ["One who wears a necklace of fingers"] An outlaw and murderer who, after an encounter with the Buddha, repented of his past misdeeds and dedicated himself to the spiritual life.

asava [Pali "flow"; Skt. *ashrava*] The outflow of attention or consciousness inherent in a conditioned mental state; passion; taint. Asava may imply the intoxication arising from selfish passions.

atman [Skt. "self"; Pali *atta*] Self, oneself. In the Upanishads and other Hindu scriptures the Atman is the spiritual Self, the "changeless in the midst of change."

avidya [*a* "not"; *vidya* "wisdom"] "Not knowing," ignorance.

bardo [Tibetan "in between state"] The period between two lives in which the soul looks back upon its previous life and also travels towards its next existence.

Bhartrihari A Sanskrit poet of the 5th century A.D. who wrote elegant verses on the themes of love, renunciation, and moral conduct.

bhikshu [Skt. "one who seeks alms"; Pali *bhikkhu*] A religious mendicant; a Buddhist monk.

Bimbisara The ruler of Magadha, who became a follower of the Buddha. He was imprisoned by his son Ajatashatru, who came under the malign influence of Devadatta.

bodhi [Skt. & Pali "awakening"] The illumination of consciousness that comes when the mind has been stilled.

bodhi tree The tree under which the Buddha attained enlightenment, in Bodh Gaya, in the modern state of Bihar. Even in the lifetime of the Buddha this site became a shrine for Buddhist pilgrims.

bodhisattva [Skt. "one whose nature is enlightenment"; Pali *bodhisatta*] One who strives to become a Buddha through many lives; the Buddha before his enlightenment. Also, one who seeks enlightenment in order to help others, one who vows to go on being reborn in order to help others.

brahmin [Skt. & Pali *brahmana*] Traditionally, a member of the priestly caste. Buddhism did not recognize caste distinctions, and in the Dhammapada a brahmin is one who has "crossed the river bravely" and reached the other shore. The twenty-sixth chapter of the Dhammapada describes the brahmin ideal, attained not through birth but through spiritual effort.

Buddha [Skt. & Pali "awakened"] One who has attained enlightenment. According to Buddhist tradition, many Buddhas have been born in the past and many more will be born in the future. The Buddha for our era is Siddhartha Gautama, born around 563 B.C.

Buddhist chronicles Commentaries and historical accounts that lie outside the Buddhist canon but are some of the earliest Buddhist sources, for example, the *Mahavamsha,* a Pali text originating in Sri Lanka in the 3rd century B.C.

Buddha-nature The Buddha principle in all beings. Some Buddhist schools describe enlightenment as a search for the inherent Buddha-nature within, to realize that "everything is Buddha-nature."

deva A god or divine being.

Devadatta A cousin of the Buddha's who joined the order of monks. He turned against the Buddha and met a tragic end. The stories of the Buddha's past lives include Devadatta as well, as he was a thorn in the side of the Buddha-to-be in life after life.

Dhammapada [Pali *dhamma* from Skt. *dharma*] A collection of
verses in twenty-six chapters compiled from the teachings
of the Buddha. It is widely believed to be in large part the
words of the Buddha himself, as remembered by his closest
disciples. It is found in the Khuddaka Nikaya of the Sutta
Pitaka (Pali Canon).

dharma [Skt. from *dhri* "to support"; Pali *dhamma*] Law,
righteousness, virtue; the Buddha's teaching or Way.

dhira A word with two meanings, "wise" and "brave," it appears
several times in the Dhammapada.

duhkha [Skt. "suffering"; Pali *dukkha*] Suffering; suffering arising
from impermanence and ignorance.

Eightfold Path The path laid out by the Buddha in his first
sermon. The eight steps are: Right Understanding, Right
Purpose, Right Speech, Right Action, Right Occupation,
Right Effort, Right Attention, and Right Meditation.

Gautama [Skt.; Pali *Gotama*] The Buddha's family name.
Siddhartha was his given name and Shakya his clan name.

Heart Sutra A short text found in the Prajnaparamita, ("The
Perfection of Wisdom"), a collection of some of the most
important scriptures in later Buddhism which form an
extensive genre of their own. The fourteen verses of the
Heart Sutra are sometimes said to contain the entire
message of the Buddha.

Jataka Tales Stories of the Buddha's former lives. These popular
stories found in the Pali Canon tell of the adventures
of the bodhisattva as he was born again and again,
sometimes as a man, sometimes as an animal, but always
cultivating virtue and continuing on his journey to
enlightenment. The Jatakas are considered some of the
earliest Buddhist scriptures, dating to the 4th century B.C.

Jetavana A park purchased by the merchant Anathapindika for the Buddha's use. The owner did not want to sell it and demanded that Anathapindika cover the ground with gold, which he did. The Buddha spent many rainy seasons here, a period when he did not travel but taught gatherings of students, both householders and monastics. It is near the town of Savatthi, mentioned many times in the Pali Canon.

Kapilavastu The city in which the Buddha grew up, though he was born nearby in Lumbini. It is not known if the ancient city was in what is today Northern India or just over the border in Nepal.

karma [Skt. "something done"; Pali *kamma*] Action; an event, physical or mental, considered as both cause and effect; the sum of what one has done, said, and thought. The law of karma states that every event is the result of a previous event and must have consequences of the same nature.

kshanikavada "The doctrine of momentariness," which states that everything is arising and dying and being reborn every moment (*kshana*). This creates a flow of existence, with each momentary entity linked to the next by karma. Normally, the mind cannot perceive this process and therefore we believe in a continuity of experience.

Kisa Gotami [Pali] A young woman of Savatthi who went to the Buddha for comfort when her child died. She became one of the foremost followers of the Buddha.

Kosambi An important city in the Buddha's time. The Vinaya Pitaka relates the story of the monks of Kosambi who could not live in harmony and how the Buddha tackled the problem.

Magadha An important kingdom in ancient India, in the region of modern Bihar. Magadha's capital city was Rajagaha, scene of many events in the Buddha's life.

Mahabharata One of the epics of India. It tells the story of a
  great dynastic war and contains much spiritual instruction
  and Hindu philosophy.

Malayalam Language of Kerala.

Mara [Skt. and Pali from *mri* "to die"] Death, "the Striker" or
  "Tempter"; embodiment of the selfish attachments and
  temptations that bind one to the cycle of birth and death.

Milinda The ruler of an Indo-Greek kingdom in the 2nd century
  B.C., called Menander in Greek sources. *The Questions
  of King Milinda* record the discussions between the king
  and the Buddhist sage Nagasena and suggest that the king
  became a follower of the Buddha.

Moggallana [Pali] One of the foremost disciples of the Buddha.
  He was born near Rajagaha and was a boyhood friend
  of the Buddha's other principal disciple, Sariputta. These
  two became known as the Twin Brethren, who were both
  important during the lifetime of the Buddha, and who
  both died before the Buddha.

Nagarjuna (2nd century A.D.) An early Mahayana Buddhist who
  developed key concepts such as shunyata and dependent
  origination into a sophisticated philosophical system.
  Nagarjuna and other Buddhist philosophers entered into
  the lively culture of debate in India, as several Buddhist
  schools began to emerge in the late centuries B.C. and
  early centuries A.D.

Nagasena The name of the Buddhist sage in the *Questions of
  King Milinda*.

nirvana [Skt.; Pali *nibbana*] Freedom from all selfish bonds;
  enlightenment. In the Dhammapada, nirvana is the
  supreme goal of all human evolution, the highest joy and
  freedom (vs. 23). Even one step on the path to nirvana is

better than any worldly attainment (vs. 178). It is the state
of peace beyond all selfish passions (vs. 226).

Pali The language of the Theravada Canon (1ˢᵗ century B.C.),
which includes the Dhammapada. It is a Middle Indo-
Aryan language, closely related to Sanskrit, that combines
several dialects used by the Buddha and his early followers
in North India. Scholars believe that the Buddha's native
language was Magadhi, but Pali includes other Middle
Indo-Aryan dialects as well because the Buddha's
teachings quickly spread beyond the region of Magadha
itself. It is also possible that the Buddha taught in various
dialects to meet the needs of his listeners. Later Buddhist
texts, such as those in the Mahayana tradition, tended to
return to the Sanskrit language. Many terms have both
a Pali and a Sanskrit form, though the Sanskrit is usually
more familiar to English speakers, e.g. *nibbana* in Pali and
nirvana in Sanskrit.

Rahula The Buddha's son. The Pali scriptures tell the touching
story of how the Buddha returned to his family after
attaining enlightenment and accepted Rahula into the
sangha.

Rajagaha [Pali] The capital of Magadha during the Buddha's
time. The Buddha visited the city many times.

Rama A prince of the ancient kingdom of Ayodhya. He is
worshipped as a form of Vishnu.

Ramayana One of the principal epics of India, it tells the story of
Rama.

saṁsara [Skt. and Pali "that which is in incessant movement"]
The cycle of birth and death; the world of change.
According to Buddhist teaching, the only thing that is not
samsara is nirvana.

samskara [Skt.; Pali *sankhara*] A deep mental impression produced by past experiences; a mental or behavioral complex; the element of personality that is the agency of karma.

sangha [Skt. & Pali "gathering"] The community of monks and nuns; the Buddhist community in general, both lay and monastic. The sangha is the third of the Three Jewels: Buddha, Dharma, and Sangha.

Sariputta [Pali] A foremost disciple of the Buddha. Sariputta, the Buddha said, kept the wheel of the dharma turning and was to be regarded as second only to the Buddha himself in wisdom.

satsang Spiritual fellowship.

Savatthi [Pali] An important city in the Buddha's time, it was the capital of the kingdom of Kosala. The Buddha visited Savatthi many times and much of his teaching was given here.

Shakya [Skt.; Pali *Sakya*] The Buddha's clan name. The Shakyas were a warrior caste that ruled a small independent kingdom centered around Kapilavastu at the time of the Buddha's birth. Later the Shakya kingdom was absorbed into the larger domain of Kosala.

shunyata [Skt.; Pali *sunnata*] "Emptiness," defined and elaborated by different Buddhist schools which teach that we may perceive a world full of separate things and beings, but in reality these things and beings are "empty" of a separate self or separate existence. In the Prajnaparamita Sutra shunyata is defined as "that which has no cause, that which is beyond thought or conception, that which is not produced, that which is not born, that which is without measure."

Siddhartha The Buddha's given name. It means "he who achieves his goal."

skandha [Skt. "heap"; Pali *khandha*] The five elements of the body-mind complex: form (the body), sensation, perception, samskara, and consciousness.

sutra (Skt.; Pali *sutta*) A Hindu or Buddhist text. In Buddhism it refers to a canonical scripture, usually a teaching attributed to the Buddha or a close disciple. In the Pali Canon, called "the three baskets," the second is the basket of sutras, the Sutta Pitaka, which contains the Dhammapada. Mahayana also uses the term *sutra* to refer to canonical teachings, such as the Heart Sutra.

Tathagata [Skt. & Pali, "one who has gone this way"] An epithet of the Buddha that he used to refer to himself. *Tatha* means "thus, so also, in like manner" and in Buddhism can mean "the truth as it really is." *Tathagata* then means one who has known the true reality of things.

tathata [Skt. & Pali] Suchness, is-ness, reality as it is without any conditioned thought imposed upon it. To see the suchness of things is to enter a mode of knowing beyond the duality of subject and object.

trishna [Skt. "thirst"; Pali *tanha*] Craving, thirst for selfish satisfaction. In the Second Noble Truth it is said that trishna is the cause of all suffering.

vairagya [Skt.; Pali *viraja*] Renunciation, detachment.

Upanishads Scriptures dealing with wisdom rather than ritual or tradition. They are a part of the Veda.

Yama [Skt. & Pali] The god of death.

Yashodhara The Buddha's wife and the mother of Rahula. Later she entered the monastic sangha. Many stories are told in the Jatakas of how Yashodhara and the Buddha were together in past lives.

◇ Notes

References are to page numbers.

25 "For those in great fear of the flood": Sutta Nipata 5 (Pali Canon)

35 "Form is foam": Samyutta Nikaya (Pali Canon)

103 "In pleasure there is fear": *Vairagya Shatakam 31*

188 Maugham's quote about meditation is from his *A Writer's Notebook*. He describes his visit to Ramana Maharshi in his essay "The Saint" in *Points of View*.

219 "Mysticism is the life of religion": D. T. Suzuki, *The Awakening of Zen*

225 "There is an unborn, an unbecome, an unmade, an uncompounded": Udana 8.3 (Pali Canon)

238 "There is no measuring of one who has disappeared": Sutta Nipata (Pali Canon)

246 "Gone, gone, gone beyond": the Heart Sutra from the Prajnaparamita, *The Perfection of Wisdom,* a Mahayana scripture translated widely throughout Asia

252 The description of the Buddha's death is taken from the Mahaparinibbana Sutta (Pali Canon).

◈ Index

◈

THE BLUE MOUNTAIN CENTER OF MEDITATION

The Blue Mountain Center of Meditation publishes Eknath Easwaran's books, videos, and audios, and offers retreats on his eight-point program of passage meditation. For more information:

The Blue Mountain Center of Meditation

Box 256, Tomales, California 94971

Telephone: +1 707 878 2369

Toll-free in the US: 800 475 2369

Facsimile: +1 707 878 2375

Email: info@easwaran.org

www.easwaran.org

blog.easwaran.org

facebook.easwaran.org

twitter.easwaran.org

youtube.easwaran.org

NILGIRI PRESS

CLASSICS OF INDIAN SPIRITUALITY SERIES

INTRODUCED AND TRANSLATED
BY EKNATH EASWARAN

THE DHAMMAPADA

This collection of the Buddha's teachings is permeated with all the power and practicality of one of the world's most appealing spiritual teachers.

THE BHAGAVAD GITA

Prince Arjuna, despairing on the battlefield of life, receives profound teachings from his spiritual guide, Sri Krishna, on life, work, love, and the immortal Self.

THE UPANISHADS

In these most ancient of Indian wisdom texts, illumined sages share flashes of insight, the result of many years of investigation into consciousness itself.

NILGIRI PRESS

Inspired by Mahatma Gandhi, Easwaran saw the Gita as "not only magnificent literature but a sure guide to human affairs – one that could throw light on the problems I faced in my own times of crisis."

This book is Easwaran's guide to the Gita, his distillation of its teachings and his answer to the questions: "What is the Gita really about? And what is its relevance for us today?" *Essence of the Bhagavad Gita* is a completely new publication based on talks that Easwaran gave to his close students towards the end of his life, after forty years of a career in which he

NILGIRI PRESS

taught, studied, and applied the principles of the Gita with a contagious enthusiasm.

As an ancient scripture, the Gita can be confusing for modern readers, so Easwaran highlights the main themes, explains the key concepts, and shares the verses he loves best, using his own translation from the original Sanskrit. Along the way, he uncovers the Gita's startling insights into the problems threatening our civilization.

Like the warrior-prince Arjuna, we must learn to make wise choices. In this modern, original interpretation Easwaran shows how the Gita points a way forward for us – both as individuals and in our global society today.

NILGIRI PRESS

ESSENCE OF THE UPANISHADS

A Key to Indian Spirituality

(*Formerly titled* Dialogue with Death)

The Katha Upanishad, one of India's classic wisdom texts, embraces all the key ideas
of Indian spirituality within the context of a
powerful mythic quest. Set in the shadowy
kingdom of Death, the Katha opens with the
young hero, Nachiketa, seeking answers to the
age-old questions: "What is the purpose of
life? And what will happen to me after I die?"
The King of Death emerges as the perfect spiritual guide – challenging, uncompromising,
and direct.

But the insights of the Katha, as with all the
Upanishads, are scattered, hard to understand.
Easwaran explains the core concepts and presents them systematically, illustrating them
through everyday examples and analogies, as
a way to explore deeper and deeper levels of
personality. Taken this way, the Katha pro-
vides a comprehensive answer to the question
"Who am I?"

NILGIRI PRESS

PASSAGE MEDITATION

*Bringing the Deep Wisdom of the Heart
into Daily Life*

In Easwaran's universal method of passage meditation, you choose a spiritual text from the world's great traditions that embodies your highest ideals. You memorize it and then send it deep into consciousness through slow, sustained attention. With regular practice, the passages become lifelines, taking you to the source of wisdom deep within and then guiding you through all the challenges of daily life.

Eknath Easwaran taught passage meditation to thousands of people for over forty years, including a course at the University of California. Meditation is supported by seven other points in Easwaran's practical spiritual program, helping you to stay calm, kind, and focused throughout the day. Thoroughly tested, consistent and clear, this book gives you all you need to start meditating.

NILGIRI PRESS

CONQUEST OF MIND

Take Charge of Your Thoughts &
Reshape Your Life Through Meditation

Getting caught in unwanted thoughts and
emotions can feel like an inevitable part of
life – but Easwaran shows how to break free.
Just as a fitness routine can result in a strong,
supple body, spiritual disciplines can shape a
secure, loving mind. With insights from the
Buddha, everyday examples, and practical exercises, Easwaran explains how we can train
the mind not just in meditation but throughout the day.

NILGIRI PRESS

Publisher's Cataloging-In-Publication Data
(Prepared by The Donohue Group, Inc.)

Eknath, Easwaran, 1910–1999.
  Essence of the Dhammapada : the Buddha's call to nirvana /
Eknath Easwaran.

  p. ; cm. -- ([The wisdom of India series ; bk. 3])

  Includes index.
  ISBN: 978-1-58638-097-7

  1. Tipitaka. Suttapitaka. Khuddakanikāya. Dhammapada-
-Criticism, interpretation, etc. 2. Nirvana. 3. Spiritual life-
-Buddhism. 4. Indian philosophy. I. Title. II. Series: Wisdom
of India (Tomales, Calif.) ; bk. 3.

BQ1377 .E27 2013
294.3/82322   2013931152